D1632324

A MARY FORD PUBLICATION

DECORATIVE
SUGAR FLOWERS
FOR CAKES

MARY
FORD

ACKNOWLEDGEMENTS

I would like to record my thanks to Pat Cockayne who produced all of the flowers in this book. It has been an enormous privilege to work with Pat, and the flowers in this book are evidence of her talent in sugarcraft.

I know that Pat has enjoyed the opportunity of working with my husband, Michael, on the arrangement of sprays and the photographic side, and I am delighted that the partnership worked so well.

Finally, my thanks are also due to Pat's husband, Allin, without whose constant support this book would not have been achieved.

PAT COCKAYNE

Pat Cockayne is an extremely creative and dedicated worker in sugarcraft. After taking six years of tuition at her local college, including time spent attending Mary Ford's classes, she began to apply her considerable talents to teaching sugarcraft.

Pat's tremendous enthusiasm and experience enabled her to reach a very high standard of craftmanship. She prides herself on her delicate floral creations and her painstaking research into precise detail. She seeks new blossoms throughout the year, taking them into her workroom to research. Her husband photographs each new acquisition before she pulls the blossoms apart petal by petal and section by section to record size and colour, and then draws the outlines of petal and component parts to keep as a permanent record of the flower's composition. This is how she is able to produce the wonderfully lifelike flowers in this book.

OTHER MARY FORD TITLES

101 CAKE DESIGNS (320 pages) – ISBN: 0 946429 00 6
CAKE MAKING & DECORATING (96 pages) – ISBN: 0 946429 41 3
THE NEW BOOK OF CAKE DECORATING (224 pages) – ISBN: 0 946429 45 6
CHILDREN'S CAKES (96 pages) – ISBN: 0 946429 35 9
QUICK & EASY CAKES (208 pages) – ISBN: 0 946429 42 1
PARTY CAKES (120 pages) – ISBN: 0 946429 13 8
SUGARCRAFT CAKE DECORATING (96 pages) – ISBN: 0 946429 30 8
CAKE RECIPES (96 pages) – ISBN: 0 946429 43 X
HOME BAKING WITH CHOCOLATE (96 pages) – ISBN: 0 946429 37 5
MAKING CAKES FOR MONEY (120 pages) – ISBN: 0 946429 44 8
THE COMPLETE BOOK OF CAKE DECORATING (256 pages) – ISBN: 0 946429 36 7
CHILDREN'S BIRTHDAY CAKES (112 pages) – ISBN: 0 946429 46 4
DESSERTS (96 pages) – ISBN: 0 946429 40 5
WEDDING CAKES (96 pages) – ISBN: 0 946429 39 1

BOOKS BY MAIL ORDER

Mary Ford operates a mail order service for all her step-by-step titles. If you write to Mary at the address below she will provide you with a price list and details. In addition, all names on the list receive information on new books and special offers. Mary is delighted, if required, to write a personal message in any book purchased by mail order.

Write to: Mary Ford, MF Books, 30 Duncliff Road, Southbourne,
Bournemouth, Dorset. BH6 4LJ. U.K.

ISBN 0 96429 51 0

©1991 Mary Ford Publications Limited.
99 Spring Road, Tyseley, Birmingham. B11 3 DJ UK.

First Published 1991
This Edition 1994

Contents

ONE of the major growth areas in sugarcraft in the last few years has been sugar flowers. My first sugar flowers book, *Sugar Flowers Cake Decorating*, was extremely well received and filled an obvious gap in the titles covered by Mary Ford publications. In recognition of both the success of that first book, and the increasing interest in the area, I am delighted to introduce this new book of superlative, hand-crafted flowers.

The interest in sugar flowers is partly due to the variety of occasions on which they can be used. For instance, it has become increasingly popular for a bride to have the flowers from her bridal spray copied for her wedding cake in order to keep them as a permanent memento of the occasion. Birthday, christening, anniversary, and other special occasion cakes, are also enhanced with these exquisite flowers. Sugar flowers will last for years if kept in airtight boxes or in the attractive glass domes that are now available. If small sprays are used on cakes, these can also be given as a pleasing remembrance to relatives or godparents. Small table arrangements can also be made and used for any occasion.

The versatility of the flowers is a crucial part of their appeal. They can be mixed with real foliage, or with specially made filler blossoms, to create sprays for decoration at times of the year when fresh flowers are scarce and expensive.

Many fresh flowers have limited colour ranges. However, by copying these flowers in paste, one can adapt to the colour scheme specifically required for the occasion. Thought must, however, be given to the natural colour of flowers and their association with the seasons. When making the daffodil, it would not be appropriate for this to be coloured blue, for example. Flowers can also be specially chosen to fit a specific colour scheme. One of the most popular flowers for almost any occasion, of course, is the rose as this can be coloured in a wide variety of shades. By keeping to the original flower's shape and colour, but adapting the scale to suit the cake, any flower can be used as required.

With time, skill, patience, and a few practical hints, beautiful flowers can be accomplished by almost anyone. With the step-by-step approach to making the flowers and leaves in this book, it will be easy to achieve excellent reproductions of the natural flower in sugar. With delicate strokes of the brush, using confectioners' dusting powders or colours, the creations can become so lifelike that it could be difficult to tell the difference between the sugar flower and the real thing.

Although these flowers are suitable for decorating any type of cake, it is nonetheless emphasised that the wires used in building the flowers should not be pushed into food products. Particular care and attention should be given to small floral sprays or blossom used on children's cakes. All wired sugar flowers should be removed prior to serving cake to children and adults.

Mary Ford

How to use this book

This book is divided into four seasons, beginning with the Spring, and each season contains instructions for making appropriate flowers. The sections commence with useful information related to the season including the relevant colours and festivals with a flower calendar for each month. A cake design is also illustrated for each season. Each flower has background information and includes the flowering period, colour and the sentiment it conveys in the language of flowers. Suggestions are given for using the flowers on seasonal and celebration cakes. In addition, instructions are included for making filler blossoms which can be incorporated into sprays or table decorations.

The preliminary section contains both recipes and important information relating to crafting the flowers and should be read before commencing work. Beginners will find this section extremely useful as it contains hints for achieving expert results with the minimum of difficulty.

Equipment

ALL the equipment used throughout this book can be purchased from most sugarcraft shops or from any of the many sugarcraft exhibitions held around the U.K. and worldwide.

Cutters: These are available in plastic or metal material, both types were used in this book.

Colours: Colours can be purchased in paste, liquid or powder form.

Knife: Any small flat knife is suitable for lifting the petals or leaves from the board.

Ball Tools: There are several types and makes of ball tool available. The one used in this book was bone-shaped.

Stamens: There are a very wide range of stamens to choose from. Care should be taken to use the right size for the particular flower being made.

Rolling Pin: There are several types of small rolling pin on the market, made in nylon or plastic material. A small board in the same material is useful for rolling out paste.

Wires: Cotton covered wires should always be used. Different gauges are available and the gauge required is specified in the step-by-step instructions for each flower.

Tape: The tape referred to in this book is ordinary florist's tape (available from most florist shops). The average width is 11mm (½"). Throughout the book, this was cut to half the width.

Flower Paste

FLOWER paste is a firm, sweet paste used for modelling hand-crafted flowers. It produces a wonderfully life-like, translucent finish which is easily coloured to create stunningly realistic blooms. This versatile medium can reproduce, with careful planning, design, colour and make-up, almost any flower which is grown today. It is possible to recreate a flower in any size and is therefore ideal for decorating tiered cakes where graduated blooms are required.

Before modelling a flower, it is useful to experiment with the various ready-made pastes available and with the different recipes for home-made pastes to test elasticity, taking of colour, drying, crusting, break-up during manipulation, etc. Each person's hands vary from the point of view of moisture and temperature and experimentation will determine the ideal paste for your own personal use. The recommended recipe in this book is based on Pat's hands. Climatic changes will also affect the paste throughout the year and it will, therefore, be necessary to adjust the moisture, increasing in summer and decreasing in winter, unless you are able to work in a temperature and humidity controlled environment.

When purchasing paste, or making your own, it is extremely important that the paste does not contain any blue colouring (to make it appear white). If a delicate shade of yellow is required, blue will turn it slightly green, and pink or red will develop a muddy brown tinge. This can be very damaging to the overall effect of the finished blossom, particularly if you are tinting to achieve realistic colours.

Patience is the most important requirement, either when experimenting or crafting the flowers. Time is essential to allow the various parts of the flowers and leaves to dry properly. Never try to hurry the drying processes. Conversely, if the paste dries out too much while you are working it will be impossible to shape. Always work on a small amount at a time, covering any pre-cut petals with plastic. Store the remaining paste in a polythene bag in the refrigerator until required. The amount of time required to produce the finished flower should be carefully calculated and allowed for in the timetable for the preparation of a celebration cake.

Making Flower Paste

RECIPE

Icing Sugar (sieved)	455g (16oz)
Gum Tragacanth	3 teaspoons
Gelatine	2 teaspoons
Cold Water	5 teaspoons
White Vegetable Fat	2 teaspoons
Liquid Glucose	2 teaspoons
Egg White	1 (size 2)

NOTE: Use Trex or Spry white vegetable fat, not lard.

Mixer Method: Follow the step-by-step instructions given below.

Alternative Kneading Method

1. Grease 2 basins with white fat (basins A and B).
2. Place half the sugar with the tragacanth into basin A, cover with dry cloth and plate. Place over pan of boiling water, gently heat until sugar is hot.
3. Heat remaining sugar in basin B over hot water.
4. Pour the water into a cup and sprinkle on the gelatine. Leave until spongy, then dissolve over hot water until clear (stir occasionally). Add fat and glucose, heat gently until dissolved.
5. Pour the mixture into basin A then quickly add egg white, stir briskly until white.
6. Briskly stir contents of basin A into B until stiff. Lightly grease hands and knead the paste until very white and pliable. Store as step **6** below.

1 Sieve the icing sugar and gum traga-canth into a bowl. Place the bowl over a saucepan of boiling water, cover with a cloth and plate. Heat gently until the sugar is warm to the touch.

2 Pour the water into a cup and sprinkle gelatine over it. Leave for 10 minutes until it becomes spongy. Place cup in a saucepan of hot water (**do not boil**) until the gelatine dissolves.

3 Add the white fat and the glucose to the melted gelatine and heat gently until dissolved.

4 Carefully separate the white from the yolk of the egg. Remove the 'string'.

5 Add all the ingredients to the warmed icing sugar. Beat on maximum with a heavy duty mixer for approximately 15-20 minutes until white and stringy.

6 Place the flower paste in a polythene bag and store in a sealed container in a refrigerator for a minimum of 24 hours before use.

Using Flower Paste

COLOURING

Flower paste should be coloured with edible paste colouring as liquid will affect the consistency of the paste. In the main, glycerine based colours are used, except where flowers naturally have a very deep strong colour. In this case, it is preferable to make the paste a pale shade of the flower's natural colour and then enhance the colour with confectioners' dusting powder when the petal is dry. When using glycerine colours, remember they are concentrated, so use sparingly. Colour should be added gradually using the end of a clean cocktail stick (see step *1*). Red and yellow colours can deepen when left to stand. The paste should be chilled after colouring to return it to a workable consistency.

Completed flowers, petals and leaves can be dusted with confectioners' dusting powder (see step *5*) or painted with liquid colours (see step *6*). Confectioners' dusting powder is ideal for delicately colouring petal edges or centres. Painting produces a more pronounced colour. When painting a petal it is essential that the paint brush be just damp with colour. If too wet a brush is used the paste may soften. Dusting and painting should only be carried out after the petals have dried.

TO COLOUR PASTE
1 Gradually add the colour to the flower paste using a cocktail stick.

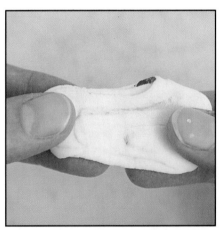

2 Mix in thoroughly by stretching and kneading the flower paste.

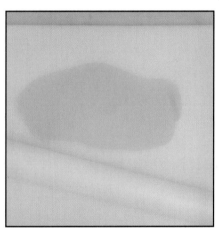

3 Roll out thinly to check that the colour is evenly mixed.

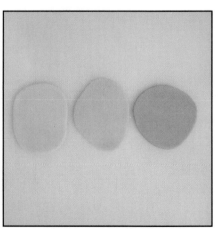

4 Picture shows 3 shades of a colour for use in flower making.

DUSTING A FLOWER
5 Brush the edges of petals with confectioners' dusting powder to highlight the petals, creating a gentle, life-like effect.

TO PAINT A PETAL
6 Paint edges of petals with edible food colouring using a clean, soft and fine artists' brush to achieve definite colours where required.

MOULDING

Small pieces of flower paste can be moulded into shapes for buds or small pulled flowers (see step *1*). Moulded cones are the first stage for making a calyx or for filler blossom (see steps *1-6*).

WIRES

The gauge of wire used is specified in the step-by-step instructions for each flower. 26 gauge has mainly been used for the flowers in this book. However, a finer gauge needs to be used for small flowers. When making larger, heavier flowers two or three thicknesses of wire can be taped together if necessary. When making single petals, the gauge depends on the thickness of the petal. The centre calyx usually requires a much thicker wire.

Wires should never be inserted directly into a cake. A small ball of sugarpaste can be used to secure the flower to the cake surface or a posy stick inserted into the cake. Wired flowers should always be removed prior to cutting and serving a cake.

MOISTENING

Throughout this book, fresh egg white has been used for moistening but, if preferred, gum arabic solution can be used. Gum arabic solution is made by mixing 1 teaspoon of gum arabic into 3 teaspoons of boiling water.

When instructed to moisten paste, this means to dampen the paste. Do not wet it.

FIXING

Stamens should be moistened and inserted into the flower-centre as instructed. Moisten individual petals and position as shown in the step-by-step guide.

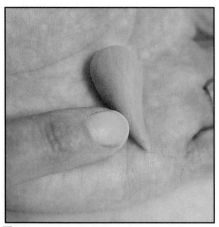

To make a calyx

1 Mould a cone of paste in the palm of the hand. (This shape can also be used for a bud or the centre of a Rose.

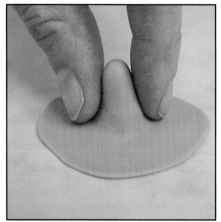

2 Spread the base of the cone and roll out, using a small rolling pin, to the shape shown.

3 Carefully position the calyx cutter over the cone and cut out the calyx shape.

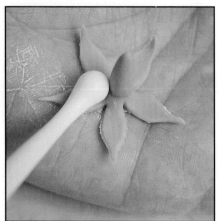

4 Immediately smooth the edge of each petal using a bone-shaped tool on the palm of the hand.

5 Moisten a hooked length of wire. Thread into the centre of the cone and pull through until the hook is firmly positioned in the centre of the calyx.

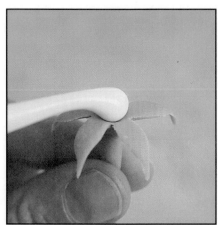

6 Press the centre of the calyx with a bone-shaped tool to form a slight indentation.

PETALS

Thinly rolled paste should be used as this achieves the most natural looking, translucent petals. The board should be very lightly greased to prevent sticking. When cutting, cut the required number of petals plus two spares. To prevent the petal edges from becoming ragged, apply sufficient pressure to the cutter to cut out cleanly. With the cutter upside down, gently pull the petal out after running a finger round the cutter edge. Cover the petals with plastic to prevent drying out. The petal edges should then be frilled or smoothed (see steps *4-6* below).

A cardboard template can be used instead of a cutter if only a few flowers are required. Place the template onto the rolled out paste and carefully cut around the template using a sharp knife. After cutting, knead the spare paste together again and re-seal.

When cutting Carnation petals, or other petals which require frilling (see step *4*), the paste should be placed on a small amount of cornflour dredged onto the board.

When making petals or leaves into which wire is inserted, leave the base of the petal slightly thicker in order to insert the wire (see steps *1-6* p.12).

When making petals on separate wires, taping the top 2.5cm (1″) of wire helps the petals to stay in place against the main wire more readily.

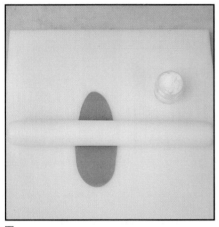

TO MAKE PETALS
1 Roll out a small piece of paste on a lightly greased board. To achieve the best results, roll as thinly as possible.

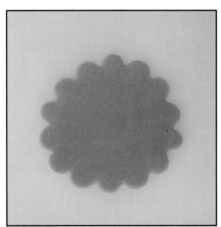

2 Using the appropriate shape cutter, carefully cut out the number of petals required.

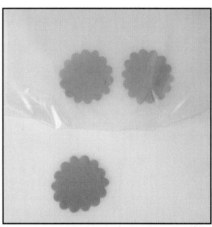

3 Always keep the petals not in use under plastic to prevent drying out.

FRILLING
4 Using a cocktail stick dipped in cornflour, carefully frill each section by rolling it backwards and forwards a little at a time.

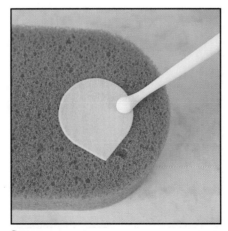

SMOOTHING
5 Place the petal on a clean household sponge and gently smooth and shape the outside petal edge with a bone-shaped tool.

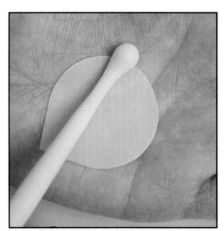

6 Alternatively, place the petal in the palm of the hand and smooth. Lightly dusted cornflour on the hands prevents moisture from softening the petal.

LEAVES

There are many varieties of leaf cutter available and if a cutter shape is not specified, an appropriate leaf should be selected for the flower being made.

Veining: Thinly roll out the paste on a greased board, leaving the paste slightly thicker at the base, and cut with the appropriate cutter. Lightly vein with a veiner if required. Alternatively, veins can be lightly scored with the end of a cocktail stick.

Wiring: Carefully insert a moistened length of wire in the base of the leaf.

Colouring: Leaves can be coloured with liquid, paste or powder colours and lightly varnished if required.

TAPE

All the flowers and leaves throughout this book have been taped using one-half the width of normal tape as this produces a much finer finish to the stem. Tape should be wound down the stem at an angle, overlapping the edges, the steeper the angle the thinner the stem.

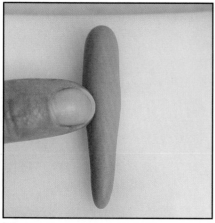

MAKING A LEAF

1 Roll out a small piece of paste into a long cone.

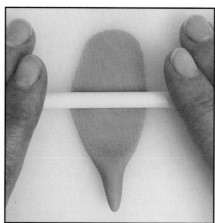

2 Roll out the top half of the cone thinly, leaving the base thicker.

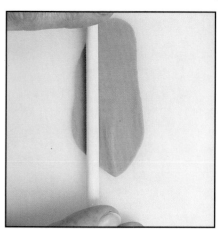

3 Roll the paste out thinly from each side of the centre leaving the central portion thicker.

4 Using the appropriate leaf cutter shape, carefully cut the leaf leaving the thicker portion at the base.

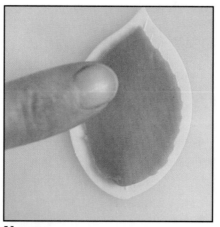

VEINING

5 Press the leaf onto a veining mould and gently peel off. Lightly smooth the edges with a bone-shaped tool.

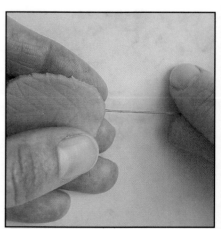

WIRING

6 Moisten a length of wire and carefully insert into the thick base of the leaf.

Making Posies and Sprays

FLORAL SPRAYS

In addition to being used as a decorative feature on a cake, sprays can also be used to create attractive place and table settings. They make an unusual decoration for a knife to cut a bridal cake. Sugar flower sprays are extremely useful in the winter-time when fresh flowers are expensive and difficult to find.

The individual flowers and filler blossom should be allowed to dry thoroughly before taping up into a spray. Begin by taping together the buds or small flowers for the top of the spray and work down the stem, adding in ribbon loops, filler blossom and larger flowers as appropriate.

FLORAL POSIES

Floral posies are seen at their best on a round cake with plenty of space around them, or as a striking table centre piece. As the shape is circular, round-shaped flowers are the easiest to work with.

Three stems of filler blossom should be taped together to form the centre. Work in a circular fashion adding ribbon loops, foliage, filler blossom and larger flowers as appropriate until the desired size is reached. Complete by adding ribbon loops and wrapping in lace. Secure the stems in a posy holder.

Spring

SPRING is the season when new life returns to the earth and this is reflected in the clear, fresh colours of the flowers and new vegetation: the soft yellows of the Daffodil, the muted mauve of the Violet and the glowing jewel-like shades of the Anemone are just a few of the flowers that bloom in the Spring.

Spring celebration cakes can be linked to the glorious theme of colour and all the citrus colours are appropriate, as are the delicate shades of Spring blossom and foliage. The vivid colouring of the brighter blooms can be used sparingly to enhance a design and create impact.

Mary created this delightful Spring Green cake decorated with seasonal blossom, Daffodils and Violets with an Easter Bunny to welcome the Spring.

SEASONAL FLOWERS

Month	March	April	May
English	Violet	Daisy	Hawthorn
Japanese	Peach	Cherry	Iris
Chinese	Tree Peony	Cherry	Magnolia

SEASONAL COLOURS

March	Soft sea-green
April	Red
May	Pink

FESTIVALS

Easter
Mothering Sunday
Cup Final Day
St David's Day   1st March
Mother-in-law Day   5th March
St Patrick's Day   17th March
Primrose Day   19th April
St George's Day   23rd April
Walpurgis Night   30th April
May Day   1st May
Anzac Day   25th April

March

1 Leek
2 Chickweed (Mouse-eared)
3 Golden Fig
4 Common Chickweed
5 Green Hellebore
6 Lent Lily
7 Early Daffodil
8 Jonquil
9 Daffodil
10 Chickweed (Upright)
11 Cornish Heath
12 Ixia
13 Heart's-ease
14 Alpine Bindweed
15 Common Coltsfoot
16 Sweet Violet
17 Shamrock
18 Leopard's Bane
19 Star of Bethlehem
20 Dog's Violet
21 Corydalis
22 Celandine
23 Peerless Daffodil
24 Golden Saxifrage
25 Marigold
26 Henbane
27 Sweet Jonquil
28 Leopard's Bane
29 Oxlip
30 Watercress
31 Benjamin-tree

April

1 Dog's Mercury
2 White Violet
3 Evergreen Alkanet
4 Red Crown Imperial
5 Yellow Crown Imperial
6 Hyacinth
7 Wood Anemone
8 Ground Ivy
9 Red Polyanthus
10 Pale Violet
11 Dandelion
12 Saxifrage
13 Green Narcissus
14 Common Borage
15 Greater Stitchwort
16 Yellow Tulip
17 Broad-leaved Arum
18 Musk Narcissus
19 Garlic
20 Spring Snowflake
21 Cypress Narcissus
22 Wood Crowfoot
23 Harebell
24 Blackthorn
25 Clarimond Tulip
26 Yellow Erysimon
27 Great Daffodil
28 Spotted Arum
29 Herb Robert
30 Cowslip

May

1 Bachelor's Button
2 Charlock
3 Peotic Narcissus
4 Gillyflower
5 Apple Blossom
6 Globe Flower
7 Asiatic Globe Flower
8 Lily of the Valley
9 Lily of the Valley
10 Peony
11 Asphodel
12 German Iris
13 Comfrey
14 Peony
15 Welsh Poppy
16 Star of Bethlehem
17 Early Red Poppy
18 Hawkweed
19 Monkshood
20 Horse Chestnut
21 Ragged Robin
22 Star of Bethlehem
23 Lilac
24 Monkey Poppy
25 Herb Bennet
26 Yellow Azalea
27 Buttercup
28 Lurid Iris
29 Bluebottle
30 Spearwort
31 Yellow Turk's-cap Lily

A

Delicate filler blossom is extremely useful for making up sprays for both cake and table decoration. When copying a bridal bouquet, the fill-in flowers can be adapted from the instructions given here to match the shape and colour of the bouquet. Each season has its own particular colours and shapes.

Although white blossom is illustrated, a wide variety of effects can be achieved simply and easily by colouring the petals in different ways. Delicately dusting the tips of the petals creates a halo of colour, whilst colouring the centre of the flower deepens its shape. Lustre colours, which impart a gentle sheen to the flower, are available in gold, silver and several soft-hued shades, and are particularly useful for wedding anniversary cakes. Petals can also be shaped from several shades of paste and arranged appropriately on the stems. Inserting coloured stamens into a white blossom can quickly transform a flower. A purple stamen creates a striking centre and the effect can be heightened by tinting the flower centre in a lighter shade.

The shape and angle of the flowers can also be varied to create different effects. Petals can be round or sharp, small or large; flowers flat or bell-shaped, open or closed. Stems can be long and delicate, or thick and chunky, and different gauges of wire can be utilised as required. By winding tape at a steep angle a thin stem is formed, winding almost horizontally produces a thicker stem. The blossoms can be clustered together or spread out along the stem.

The overall shape of the finished arrangement may require several different sizes and lengths of filler blossom sprays and the effect should be carefully planned before commencing work, with particular attention given to the placing of the flowers specific to the occasion. The main flowers should always be made first. The wedding cake illustrated on page 43 provides a beautiful example of the combination of large, dominant flowers with delicate filler blossom.

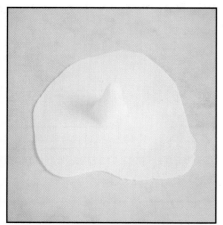

1 Make a cone from paste. Flatten out the base, as shown, using a small rolling pin.

2 Using cutter shape **A**, carefully place over the cone and cut the base to form petals.

3 Moisten the tip of a stamen and insert into centre of cone. Make several blossoms and when dry tape together on 26 gauge wire to form sprigs.

Daffodil

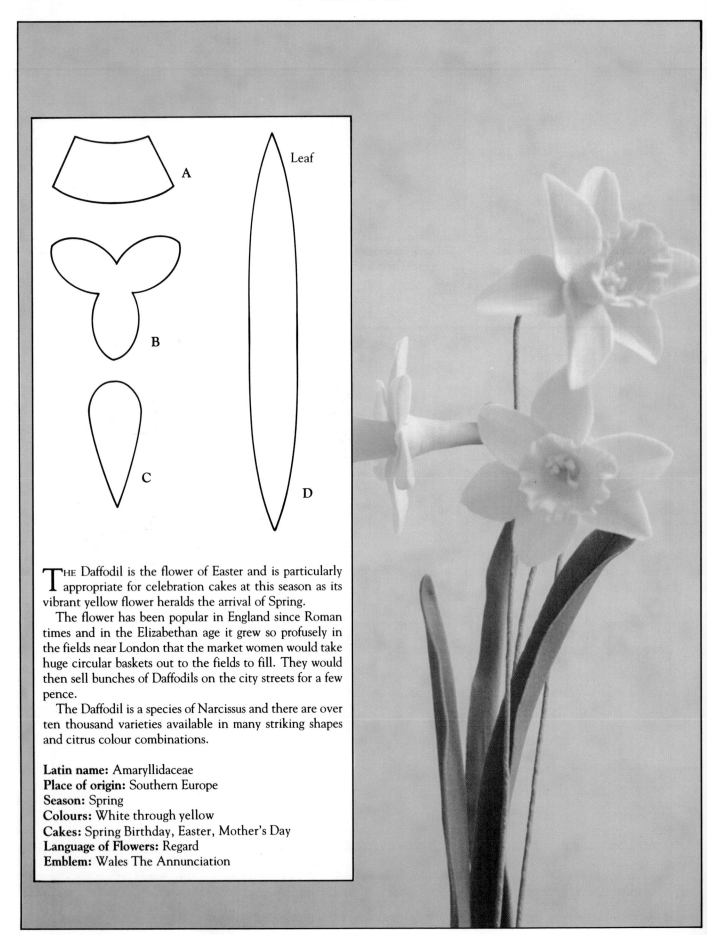

A

B

Leaf

C

D

THE Daffodil is the flower of Easter and is particularly appropriate for celebration cakes at this season as its vibrant yellow flower heralds the arrival of Spring.

The flower has been popular in England since Roman times and in the Elizabethan age it grew so profusely in the fields near London that the market women would take huge circular baskets out to the fields to fill. They would then sell bunches of Daffodils on the city streets for a few pence.

The Daffodil is a species of Narcissus and there are over ten thousand varieties available in many striking shapes and citrus colour combinations.

Latin name: Amaryllidaceae
Place of origin: Southern Europe
Season: Spring
Colours: White through yellow
Cakes: Spring Birthday, Easter, Mother's Day
Language of Flowers: Regard
Emblem: Wales The Annunciation

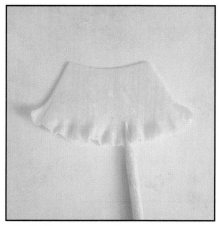

1 Roll out paste and cut using cutter shape **A**. Frill the long edge using a cocktail stick.

2 To form a trumpet, roll the frilled paste around a small tube. Moisten and join edges. Leave to dry for 24 hours.

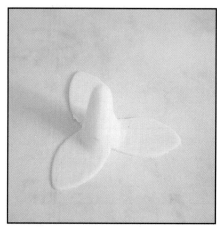

3 Make a cone from paste. Flatten base with small rolling pin. Using cutter shape **B**, cut petals leaving cone in the centre. Place on clean sponge and flatten edge.

4 Shape and vein (see p.12) each petal, then curl up as shown. Moisten hooked 24 gauge wire and insert through the cone.

5 Roll out more paste and, using cutter shape **B**, cut a petal shape.

6 Again using the sponge as a base, ball, shape and vein the petals.

7 Moisten and fix the petals to top of petals on wire. Then make a hole in the flower's centre.

8 Moisten centre and gently press trumpet onto the petals.

9 Moisten and fix 4 short pale lemon stamens, together with one long stamen (with deeper coloured tip) to centre of flower.

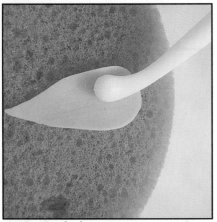

10 Cut bud casing using cutter shape **C**. Smooth, vein and shape.

11 Moisten casing and immediately fix to the back of the daffodil by wrapping the pointed end around the base of the flower.

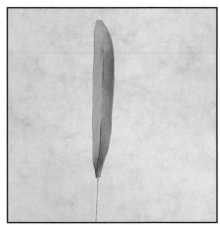

12 Roll out and cut leaves, using cutter shape **D**, to length required. Vein, shape and insert moistened 24 gauge wire well into each leaf (see p. 12).

Dianthus

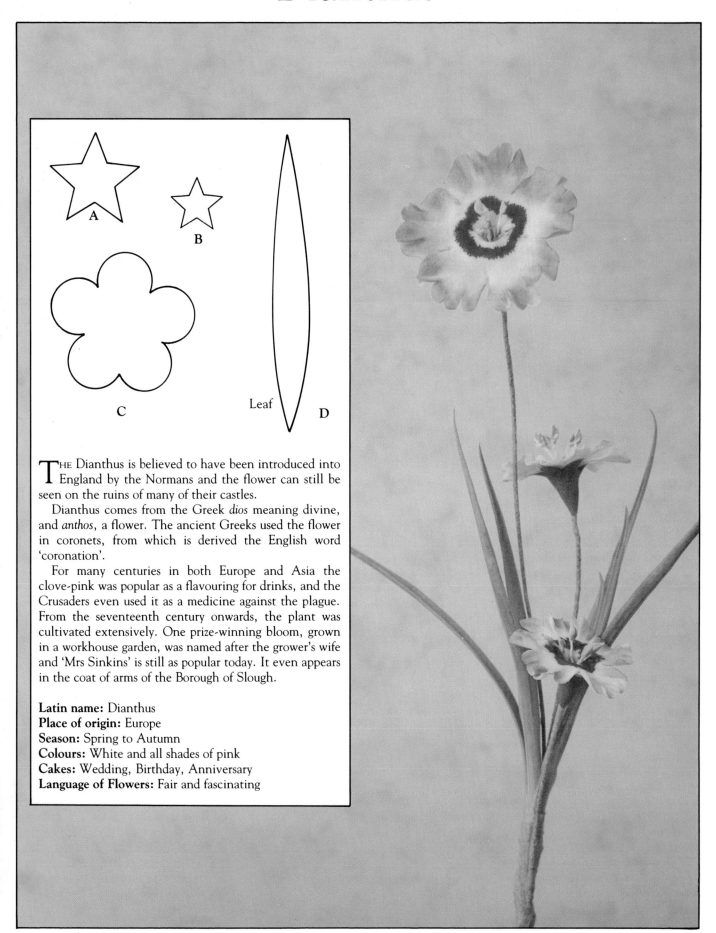

A

B

C

Leaf   D

THE Dianthus is believed to have been introduced into England by the Normans and the flower can still be seen on the ruins of many of their castles.

Dianthus comes from the Greek *dios* meaning divine, and *anthos*, a flower. The ancient Greeks used the flower in coronets, from which is derived the English word 'coronation'.

For many centuries in both Europe and Asia the clove-pink was popular as a flavouring for drinks, and the Crusaders even used it as a medicine against the plague. From the seventeenth century onwards, the plant was cultivated extensively. One prize-winning bloom, grown in a workhouse garden, was named after the grower's wife and 'Mrs Sinkins' is still as popular today. It even appears in the coat of arms of the Borough of Slough.

Latin name: Dianthus
Place of origin: Europe
Season: Spring to Autumn
Colours: White and all shades of pink
Cakes: Wedding, Birthday, Anniversary
Language of Flowers: Fair and fascinating

TO MAKE A BUD

1 Make a cone from paste and insert a moistened hooked length of 26 gauge wire to form bud centre. Leave to dry for 24 hours.

2 Make a cone of paste and gently flatten the base. Using cutter shape A cut out base to form the outer leaves. Hollow out the centre.

3 Slightly moisten the inside of the leaves, insert the wired bud and fold in the points around the centre to form the bud.

4 Cut a calyx from paste using cutter shape B. Moisten the centre and fix to base of bud. Leave to dry for 24 hours.

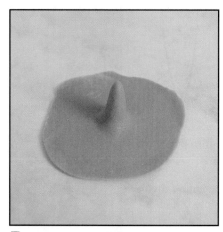

TO MAKE A FLOWER

5 Make a cone of paste and gently flatten the edges. Using cutter shape A, cut the calyx leaving cone in the centre.

6 Fix the calyx onto a moistened hooked length of 26 gauge wire. Leave to dry for 24 hours.

7 Roll out paste and cut the petals, using cutter shape C. Make small cuts in each petal, as shown.

8 Using a little cornflour, roll and frill the edges with a cocktail stick (see p.11).

9 Moisten top of calyx and fix petal in centre. Make a small hole in the centre of the petal. Leave to dry for 24 hours.

10 Paint a deep colour around centre of petal with edible food colouring using a clean, fine artists' brush.

11 Moisten the hole previously made in the centre. Insert and fix 5 pale brown stamens.

12 Dust the outer edge of the petals with confectioners' dusting powder.

Freesia

T<small>HE</small> distinctively scented Freesia is named after the German physician Frederick Heinrick Theodore Freese, who discovered it in South Africa in 1876. The orange variety is especially fragrant, but all the colours have a delicate perfume.

It is an extremely popular flower for bridal bouquets as it is available in many hues and blends into most colour schemes. It is also a useful flower for making centre pieces and place settings as it can be matched to the table linen or to the colour of the cake.

Latin name: Freesia Refracta
Place of origin: South Africa
Season: Spring and throughout the year
Colours: White, mauve, yellow and variegated
Cakes: Wedding, Anniversary

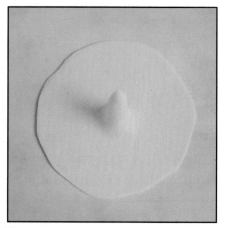

TO MAKE A FLOWER

1 Make a cone from yellow paste and gently flatten the base as shown.

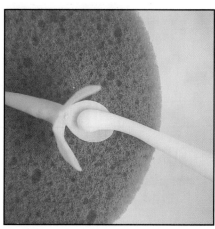

*2 Place cutter shape **A** over the cone and cut. Smooth each petal to a deep curve.*

3 Push a moistened hooked length of 24 gauge wire through the centre of the cone.

*4 Roll out yellow paste and cut another set of petals using cutter shape **A**. Smooth and shape petals, moisten and fix them into centre of cone petals.*

5 Moisten and fix 1 long stamen and 4 short stamens into flower centre.

*6 Roll out green paste and cut a small calyx using cutter shape **B**. Moisten calyx centre, insert wire and fix to the base of the cone.*

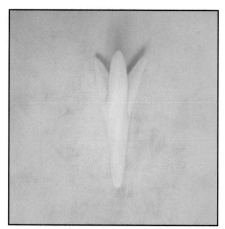

TO MAKE A CLOSED BUD

7 Make cone of paste, cutting it twice with a pair of scissors. Open out slightly to form 3 petals.

*8 Twist the 3 petals together to complete the closed bud. Using cutter shape **B**, cut out, moisten and fix a calyx to the base.*

TO MAKE A YELLOW UNOPENED BLOSSOM

*9 Moisten and insert hook shaped 28 gauge wire into cone shaped paste. Make 3 grooves to represent petals. Follow steps **11-12**.*

TO MAKE A GREEN OPENING BUD

10 Form a cone of paste and insert a moistened hooked length of 28 gauge wire to make a bud centre.

11 Using cutter shape **C**, make a large calyx. Moisten centre, insert wire and wrap around the bud centre to almost enclose it.

12 Using cutter shape **B**, cut a small calyx, moisten and insert wire through centre and fix to base of bud.

Sweet Pea

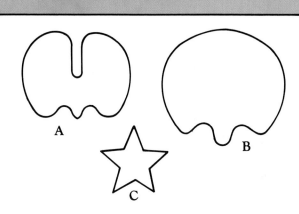

THE fragrant wild Sweet Pea was discovered in Sicily in 1697 by a monk, Father Franciscus Cupani, and sent to a schoolmaster friend in England who cultivated it.

A century later it became very popular with Queen Alexandra, who used it extensively as a cut flower and it was much loved by the Edwardians.

Sweet Peas are characterised by a large spreading petal at the back, and two wings in front which join to form the centre 'keel' and it has been likened to a tiny ship in full sail.

Latin name: Lathyrus Odoratus
Place of origin: Italy
Season: Winter through to Summer
Colours: Pink, mauve, salmon, orange, scarlet, blue and lilac
Cakes: Birthday, Mother's Day, Anniversary, Retirement
Language of Flowers: Departure and Adieu

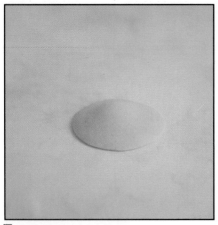

TO MAKE A HALF-OPEN FLOWER

1 Make a round ball from paste and flatten to form a domed shape.

2 Moisten the flat side of the dome. Fold in half, wrapping it around a length of 26 gauge wire to make flower centre.

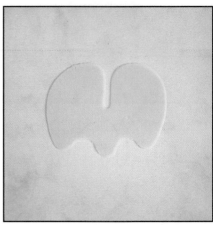

*3 Using cutter shape **A**, cut the first, small petals.*

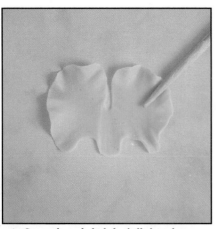

4 Smooth and slightly frill the edge using a cocktail stick (see p. 11).

5 Moisten and fix to the back of the flower centre and then fold around the sides.

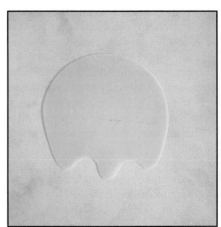

TO MAKE A FULL BLOOM

*6 Repeat steps **1-5**. Using cutter shape **B** cut a second, larger petal.*

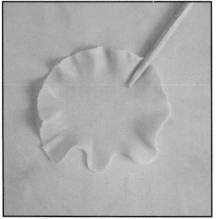

7 Smooth and slightly frill the edges using a cocktail stick (see p. 11).

8 Moisten and fix petal to the back of the flower and shape as shown.

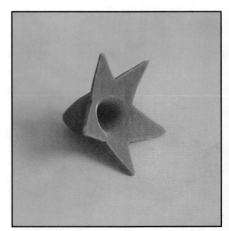

*9 Mould paste to a cone. Roll edges and cut the calyx using cutter shape **C**. Hollow out the centre.*

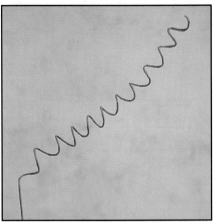

10 Moisten the centre of the calyx and insert wire stem. Fix into position around base of flower. Leave to dry for 24 hours.

11 Dust the petals using confectioners' dusting powder in a deeper shade of base colour.

12 Make the tendrils by twisting 33 gauge green wire round a pencil. Tape flowers and tendrils together to form a spray.

Daisy

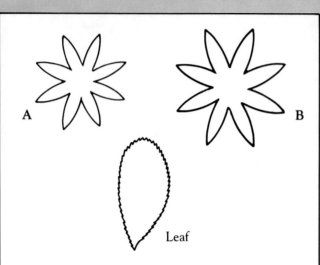

A   B

Leaf

IN France the Daisy is called the 'Marguerite' after St Margaret, the patron saint of Herbalists, and in Scotland it is known as 'Bairnwort', which means the children's flower. It is a perennial favourite with children, who have traditionally made Daisy chains to garland themselves, and with young maidens who pulled the petals off whilst reciting the old rhyme 'he loves me, he loves me not'.

There are many varieties of Daisy grown in gardens today from the humble 'weed' which is found in lawns to more exotic blooms. One of the most common is the Ox-Eye, which is also known as the Moon Daisy as its large, white face looks just like the full moon shining in the evening. The common Daisy is a well loved sight in meadows, with its attractive bright yellow centre and ray of pink-tipped white petals.

Latin name: Bellis Perennis
Place of origin: Meadowland
Season: Spring and Summer
Colour: White
Cakes: Children's
Language of Flowers: Purity of thought
Emblem: Innocence

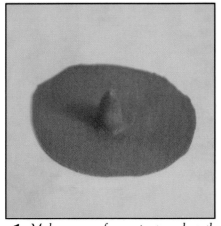

1 Make a cone of green paste and gently flatten the edges. Using cutter shape **A** cut a calyx and hollow out the centre.

2 Thin petals and insert a moistened hooked length of 26 gauge wire through the centre.

3 Cut 2 rows of petals from thinly rolled paste using cutter shape **B**.

4 Carefully cut each petal in half as shown.

5 Using a cocktail stick, thin and curl each petal.

6 Moisten and fix first row of petals onto calyx.

7 Moisten and fix second row of petals in place, as shown.

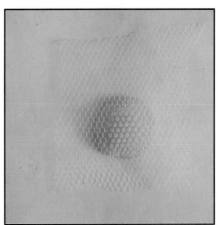

8 Make a small ball of yellow paste. Press fine net onto the ball to form the stamens. Carefully remove net.

9 Moisten and fix ball into centre of petals. Leave to dry 24 hours. Brush the centre with yellow dusting powder.

10 Dust back of petals with pale pink dusting powder.

11 Lightly dust the front edges of the petals.

12 Make a leaf from green paste, vein and insert moistened length of 26 gauge wire (see p. 12).

Anemone

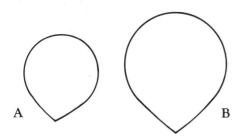

A   B

THE gentle Anemone's name comes from the Greek word *amenos*, meaning wind and this beautiful flower is also known as the wind flower.

In Greek mythology, Anemone was a beautiful nymph at the flower-goddess's court. Unfortunately she fell in love with Zephyr, the west wind, and was exiled by his jealous wife. When she died of a broken heart, Venus, the goddess of love, changed her to the anemone flower as it returns to life again in the Spring. The poor girl's misfortunes were not yet over, however, as she was abandoned to the 'rude caresses' of Boreas, the north wind, whom she could not love. Annoyed, he pulled her petals open clumsily and caused her to fade.

In slightly more recent times the Anemone is said to have sprung from the blood of Christ, at the foot of the Cross. It was also said to spring from the blood of martyrs, and pilgrims carried the seeds all over Europe.

Latin name: Ranunculaceae Anemone Coronaria
Place of Origin: Greece and Eastern Mediterranean
Season: Spring
Colours: Various shades of red and mauve
Cakes: Birthday
Language of Flowers: Forsaken

1 Make a small ball of black paste and slightly flatten the top.

2 Moisten the end of small black stamens and push into centre of ball.

3 Add 2 layers of black stamens around the outside. Tape 3 lengths of 24 gauge wire together, moisten end and insert into base of ball. Leave to dry for 24 hours.

4 Using cutter shape **A**, make 4 petals. Cover with plastic.

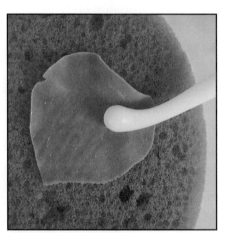

5 Smooth, shape and vein back of petal with a bone tool, as shown.

6 Moisten base of first petal and fix, as shown.

7 Repeat steps **5-6** for the remaining 3 petals.

8 Using cutter shape **B**, make 11 petals. Smooth, shape, vein and fix behind first layer, overlapping them slightly, as shown.

9 Back view shows overlapping petals. Leave to dry for 24 hours.

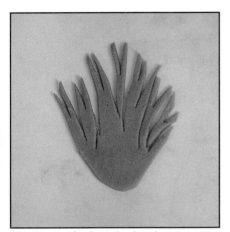

10 Cut leaf out freehand. After cutting, slightly smooth leaf to remove the 'cut edge' look. Make 3 leaves for each flower. Insert 26 gauge moistened wire.

11 Dust leaves and petals with confectioners' dusting powder. Paint centre if desired. Assemble as shown and tape into position (see p. 13).

12 Flower shows painted markings. Each flower should be slightly different.

A

B   Leaf

SHAKESPEARE mentions the humble Violet no less than eighteen times in his plays and this delicate flower has always been dear to English hearts. Its appeal is not confined to England, however. It was grown in ancient Greece for its perfume and sweetening properties.

The perfume and taste of the Violet has long been prized. The blossoms were strewn on the floor of dwellings and in clothes to scent them sweetly, and the breath was freshened with crystallized Violets. The perfume was a particular favourite of Queen Elizabeth I. Queen Victoria also loved Violets and always wore a posy of them.

Latin name: Viola Odorata
Place of origin: Europe and Britain
Season: Early Spring
Colours: Shades of mauve and white
Cakes: Mother's Day, Birthday
Language of Flowers: Modesty
Emblem: French Bonapartists

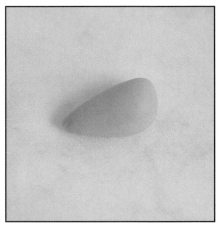

1 Make a cone from paste.

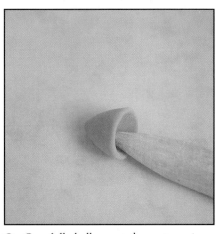

2 Carefully hollow out the centre using a cocktail stick.

3 Cut a petal one-third of the circumference wide. Cut the remainder into 4 equal petals (5 petals in all).

4 Carefully open out all the petals as shown. Using a cocktail stick, make a small hole in the centre.

5 Using a bone tool, thin and shape the petals as shown. Curl the petals on either side of the large petal inwards towards the centre.

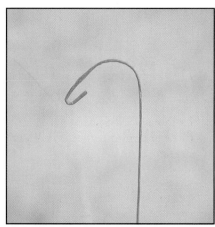

6 Bend a length of 26 gauge wire to the shape shown.

7 Moisten the wire and carefully insert into the top of the flower as shown. Moisten and insert a yellow stamen into the flower centre. Leave to dry for 24 hours.

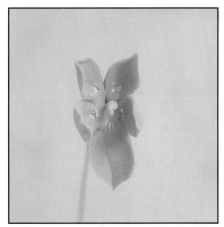

8 Using a clean, fine artists' brush and edible food colouring, paint on the centre markings as shown.

9 Using cutter shape **A**, cut out a calyx. Make a cut to the centre as shown.

10 Moisten the centre of the calyx and insert stem. Mould the calyx around the flower as shown.

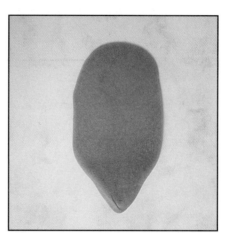

11 Cut a leaf freehand, following shape **B**, ensure that the paste at the base of the leaf is thicker.

12 Shape with a bone tool and vein with a veiner or a cocktail stick. Insert moistened 26 gauge wire into base of leaf.

Carnation

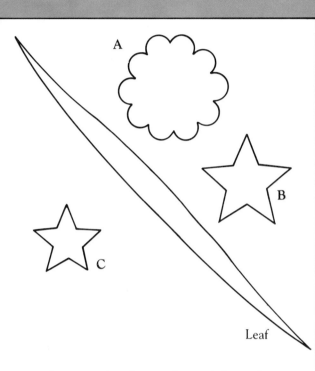

A

B

C

Leaf

THE Carnation has been cultivated for at least two thousand years. The name is derived from the Latin *carvis* meaning flesh, and the flower is found throughout Southern Europe.

Legend has it that the flower first appeared from the tears of the Virgin Mary on her way to Calvary but it was actually mentioned in the third century b.c. by the Greek writer Theophrastus, who called it 'the Divine Flower'. However, its link with mother-love has continued down the centuries and the pink Carnation is the American emblem of Mother's Day.

According to Chaucer the plant was extensively cultivated in England in the Middle Ages, having been brought to England at the time of the Norman Conquest. The name Carnation was first used by Henry Lyte in 1578 in reference to its use as a garland or coronation flower.

Latin name: Dianthus Caryophyllus
Place of origin: Southern Europe
Season: Spring and Summer
Colours: All shades of pink, peach, yellow, red, white
Cakes: Mother's Day, Wedding, Birthday, Anniversary
Language of Flowers: Red — admiration and marriage
    Pink — motherhood
    White — pure love
    Yellow — rejection
Emblem: Mother's Day

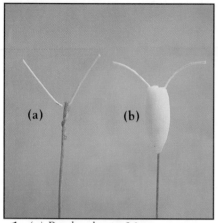

1 *(a) Bend and twist 26 gauge wire around centre of stamen. (b) Mould a paste cone. Moisten joint and insert into cone, shaping as shown. Leave to dry 24 hours.*

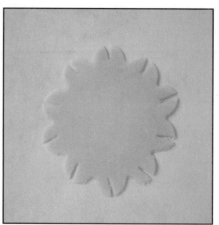

2 *Using cutter shape **A**, roll out and cut petals from thinly rolled paste. Carefully cut each petal in half as shown.*

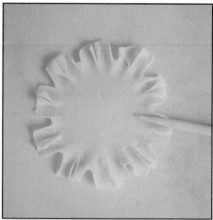

3 *Frill the edges of the petal by rolling a cocktail stick backwards and forwards, a little at a time, until well frilled.*

4 *Moisten the centre of the petal and insert wire. Fold the petal in half and fix around cone as shown.*

5 *Moisten and fold the right side of the petal to the centre as shown.*

6 *Moisten and fold the other side of the petal to the centre back and gently shape to form centre of flower.*

7 *Repeat steps **2-3** to form another petal. Moisten centre and insert wire. Shape up around the centre to start forming the flower.*

8 *Repeat steps **2-3** to form another petal. Moisten centre and insert wire. Mould the petal upwards to fan out beneath the previous petals. Leave to dry for 24 hours.*

9 *Mould a cone to form a seed pod and, using cutter shapes **B** and **C**, cut 2 calyxes from thinly rolled paste.*

10 Moisten wire and insert through seed pod. Moisten centres of large and small calyxes and insert wire stem. Mould to shape. Leave to dry for 24 hours.

11 Carefully brush the petals with confectioners' dusting powder using a clean, fine and dry artists' brush.

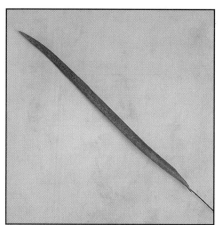

12 Cut a long, thin paste leaf. Moisten and insert end of a length of 33 gauge wire. Shape leaf with a suitable modelling tool and then vein the centre.

Summer

Summer provides a multitude of flowers in virtually every hue and shape from the delicate Honeysuckle to the flamboyant Lily and the exotic Passion Flower. With a little imagination, the cake-decorator can create cakes to suit the mood of every summer celebration. The subtle summer colours harmonise beautifully with floral artistry and the more exuberant colours of some seasonal blossoms can create a dramatic effect on a cake for a special occasion.

Roses have always been the most popular flower for wedding cakes but this versatile flower can be used for almost every occasion, particularly as its wide range of colours will blend into any colour scheme. In the cake illustrated here, cream Roses with a light dusting of pink have been used in posies to decorate a stunningly simple summer wedding cake. The posies also include beautiful cream Carnations with delicate pink petal edges, white Daisies and filler flowers.

Seasonal Flowers

Month	June	July	August
English	Honeysuckle	Water Lily	Poppy
Japanese	Wistaria	Morning Glory	Lotus
Chinese	Pomegranate	Lotus	Pear Blossom

Seasonal Colours

June   Lemon Yellow
July   Green
August   Golden Yellow

Festivals

Father's Day   June
Alexandra Rose Day   June
Summer Solstice   21st June
Midsummer Day   24th June
Orange Day   12th July
Canada Day   July
Independence Day   4th July
Australia Day   26th June

June

1 Yellow Rose
2 Common Pimpernel
3 Rose of Meaux
4 Indian Pink
5 China Rose
6 Common Pink
7 Red Centaury
8 Moneywort
9 Barberry
10 Yellow Iris
11 Midsummer Daisy
12 White Dog Rose
13 Garden Ranunculus
14 Sweet Basil
15 Sensitive Plant
16 Moss Rose
17 Yellow Money Flower
18 Horned Poppy
19 La Julienne de Nuit
20 Doubtful Poppy
21 Viper's Bugloss
22 Canterbury Bell
23 Ladies' Slipper
24 St John's Wort
25 Sweet William
26 Alpine Snowthistle
27 St John's Wort
28 Blue Cornflower
29 Yellow Rattle
30 Yellow Cistus

July

1 Agrimony
2 White Lily
3 Common Mallow
4 Tawny Day Lily
5 Double Yellow Rose
6 Hawkweed
7 Nasturtium
8 Evening Primrose
9 Marsh Sowthistle
10 Speckled Snapdragon
11 Yellow Lupine
12 Great Snapdragon
13 Blue Lupine
14 Red Lupine
15 Cape Marigold
16 Convolvulus
17 Sweet Pea
18 Autumn Marigold
19 Golden Hawkweed
20 Dragon's-head
21 Philadelphian Lily
22 African Lily
23 Musk Flower
24 Lupine Tree
25 Herb Christopher
26 Chamomile
27 Loosestrife
28 Mountain Groundsel
29 Red Chironia
30 White Mullein
31 Yellow Mullein

August

1 Thorn Apple
2 Tiger Lily
3 Hollyhock
4 Bluebell
5 Water Lily
6 Meadow Saffron
7 Amaranth
8 Love-lies-bleeding
9 Yellow Ragwort
10 Balsam
11 China Aster
12 Corn Sowthistle
13 Groundsel
14 Zinnia
15 Virgin's Bower
16 Belladonna Lily
17 Snapdragon
18 African Marigold
19 Cat's-tail Grass
20 Dandelion
21 French Marigold
22 Timothy Grass
23 Common Tansy
24 Tall Sunflower
25 Perennial Sunflower
26 Amaryllis
27 Hedge Hawkweed
28 Golden Rod
29 Yellow Hollyhock
30 Guernsey Lily
31 Pheasant's Eye

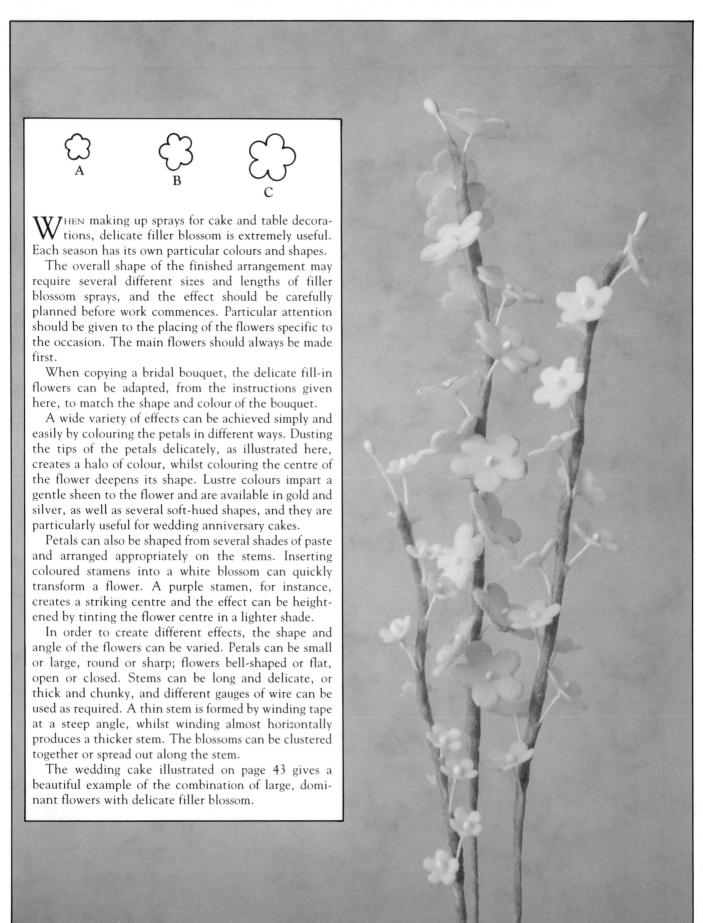

W HEN making up sprays for cake and table decorations, delicate filler blossom is extremely useful. Each season has its own particular colours and shapes.

The overall shape of the finished arrangement may require several different sizes and lengths of filler blossom sprays, and the effect should be carefully planned before work commences. Particular attention should be given to the placing of the flowers specific to the occasion. The main flowers should always be made first.

When copying a bridal bouquet, the delicate fill-in flowers can be adapted, from the instructions given here, to match the shape and colour of the bouquet.

A wide variety of effects can be achieved simply and easily by colouring the petals in different ways. Dusting the tips of the petals delicately, as illustrated here, creates a halo of colour, whilst colouring the centre of the flower deepens its shape. Lustre colours impart a gentle sheen to the flower and are available in gold and silver, as well as several soft-hued shapes, and they are particularly useful for wedding anniversary cakes.

Petals can also be shaped from several shades of paste and arranged appropriately on the stems. Inserting coloured stamens into a white blossom can quickly transform a flower. A purple stamen, for instance, creates a striking centre and the effect can be heightened by tinting the flower centre in a lighter shade.

In order to create different effects, the shape and angle of the flowers can be varied. Petals can be small or large, round or sharp; flowers bell-shaped or flat, open or closed. Stems can be long and delicate, or thick and chunky, and different gauges of wire can be used as required. A thin stem is formed by winding tape at a steep angle, whilst winding almost horizontally produces a thicker stem. The blossoms can be clustered together or spread out along the stem.

The wedding cake illustrated on page 43 gives a beautiful example of the combination of large, dominant flowers with delicate filler blossom.

1 Roll out and cut paste, using cutter **A**, **B** or **C**, to make petal shape shown. Smooth each petal edge with a bone-shaped tool on a household sponge.

2 Insert a stamen into centre of flower and moisten to fix. Tape blossoms to 26 gauge wire to form 1 stem. Leave to dry for 24 hours. Make sizes and quantity as required.

3 Brush the edge of each petal with confectioners' dusting powder. Tape together to form sprigs.

Hybrid Rose

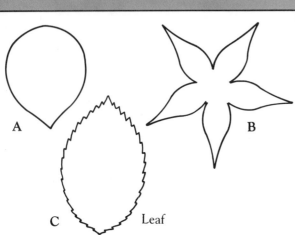

A

B

C   Leaf

THE Rose is known from American fossil evidence to be at least thirty-five million years old and it was grown extensively in the hanging gardens of Babylon over five thousand years ago.

Poets have always loved Roses and mythology assigned the Rose as the symbol of beauty, youth and love. According to Greek myth a beautiful nymph died and was transformed into a flower of unsurpassed beauty—the Rose.

Roses have always been linked to weddings. Crowns of Roses were placed on the bridal couple, who were showered with confetti in the form of rose petals.

The Hybrid Rose was, however, a very recent development produced in the mid-nineteenth century by crossing the marvellously scented but short blooming yellow and orange Persian Rose with the long-lasting Chinese Roses, and combining these with the hardy Old English red, white and pink flowers. The result was the breathtaking array of colours available today.

Latin name: Rosaceae
Place of origin: Worldwide
Season: Spring and Summer
Colours: All
Cakes: Valentine, Wedding, Anniversary, Birthday, All celebration
Language of Flowers: Love and beauty
    Bridal — happy home
    Red and white — unity
    Rosebud — youth
    Full blown — I love you
    Pink — perfect happiness
    White — innocence
    Yellow — jealousy
Emblem: Red — House of Lancaster
         White — House of York
         England

1 Mould a piece of paste to form a cone. Bend 26 gauge wire to hook shape, moisten and insert into cone. Leave to dry 24 hours.

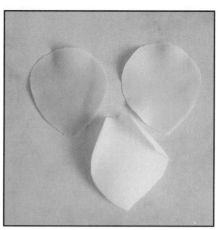

2 Mix pieces of paste to three shades of one colour, as shown. 7 dark, 3 medium and 5 light coloured petals are required, using cutter shape **A**.

3 Thin the outside edge of dark petal with a bone tool. Moisten and wrap dark petal around cone.

4 Moisten and fix 2 petals to each side of the first petal and interleave, keeping the top slightly open.

5 Repeat step *4* once more. Moisten and fix each petal to one side of the previous petal, keeping the tops slightly open.

6 Repeat step *4* once more. Moisten and fix each petal to one side of the previous petal, keeping the tops and sides open as shown.

7 Add 3 more petals, using the medium coloured paste. Equally space each petal around the flower, and then open out and shape as shown.

8 Add 5 more petals, using the palest colour paste. Equally space petals around the flower and open as shown. Leave to dry for 24 hours.

9 Mould a cone to form seed pod. Roll out separate pieces of white and green paste. Fix together and cut out calyx using a cutter shape **B**. Cut edges as shown.

10 Moisten the centre of the calyx and insert the wire through the centre. Then moisten and fix seed pod as shown. Leave to dry for 24 hours.

11 Lightly dust the rose with confectioners' dusting powder using a clean, dry and fine artists' brush.

12 Roll out, cut and vein leaves using a cutter shape **C**. Insert moistened 33 gauge wire. Leave to dry for 24 hours then dust and varnish leaves as required.

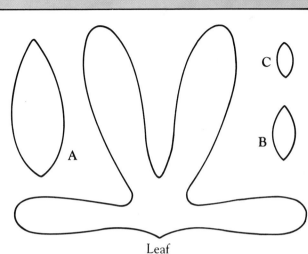

Leaf

THE Passion Flower was introduced into England by missionaries from Brazil in 1699 although its soothing herbal properties and its exotic appearance were well known before that as an illustration appeared in Parkinson's 1629 gardening book *Paradisi in Sole Paradisus Terrestris*, with a description obtained from the Jesuits.

The flower is believed to depict all the elements of Christ's Passion. The crown above the petals represents the crown of thorns; the three styles, the nails; the five stamens, Christ's wounds; the ovary, the sponge soaked in vinegar; and the ten sepals and petals symbolise the faithful apostles—Peter, who denied Christ, and Judas, who betrayed him, being omitted. The outer corona represents the countless disciples.

Latin name: Passiflora Caerulea
Place of origin: Brazil
Season: Summer/Autumn
Colour: White
Cakes: Easter
Language of Flowers: Faith and Piety
Emblem: Christ's Passion

1 Tape 3 lengths of fine wire to 2 lengths of 24 gauge wire to form stamens. Colour wires brown with edible food colouring.

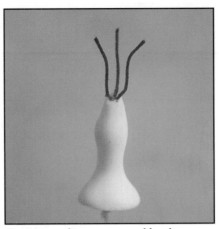

2 Using white paste, mould a shape as shown. Insert moistened wire through the centre.

3 Make 3 tiny heart-shaped pieces in brown paste and place each one on a moistened stamen.

4 Paint main part of moulded shape green using edible food colouring.

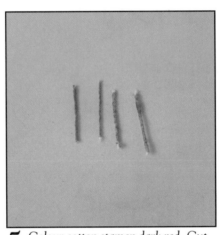

5 Colour cotton stamen dark red. Cut into 0.6cm (¼") lengths.

6 Moisten stamens and carefully fix around base, as shown.

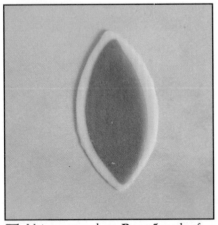

7 Using cutter shape **B** cut 5 ovals of yellow paste. Using cutter shape **C** cut 5 ovals of green paste. Moisten and fix as shown. Leave to dry for 24 hours.

8 Cut 0.6cm (¼") strips of green paste and bend as shown (5 required). Leave to dry for 24 hours.

9 Moisten one end of a strip and fix to an oval. Repeat for the remaining 4 sets. Leave to dry for 24 hours.

10 Moisten and fix oval shapes into position as shown.

11 Top view shows completed stem assembly.

12 Using white paste, mould shape as shown. Make centre hole with wire from stem assembly. Leave to dry for 24 hours.

13 Cut 5 petals in white paste using cutter shape **A**. Smooth, shape and vein.

14 Moisten back of moulded shape and fix petals as shown. Make hole in centre of petals with wire from stem assembly.

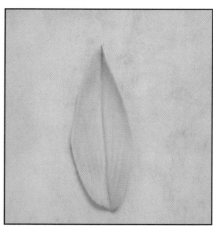

15 Roll out very thin pieces of white and green paste. Place green on top of white and roll again. Cut 5 petals using cutter shape **A**. Smooth, shape and vein.

16 Moisten and fix to back of white petals as shown.

17 Gently lift the petals from the sponge and upturn onto a suitable tray, as shown. Leave to dry for 24 hours.

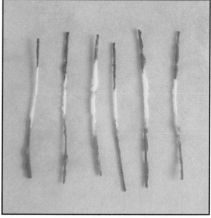

18 Cut cotton stamens into 2cm (¾") lengths and colour as shown.

19 Moisten stamens and fix around centre of petal assembly.

20 Moisten stem assembly and insert through the centre of petal assembly.

21 Carefully position to complete the flower.

Peruvian Lily

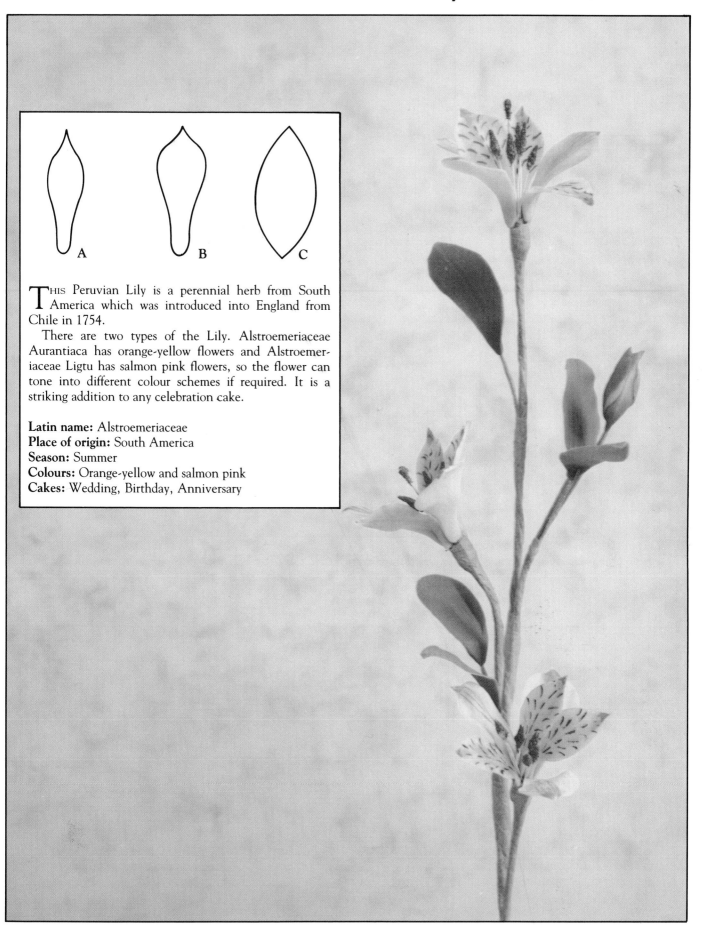

T HIS Peruvian Lily is a perennial herb from South America which was introduced into England from Chile in 1754.

There are two types of the Lily. Alstroemeriaceae Aurantiaca has orange-yellow flowers and Alstroemeriaceae Ligtu has salmon pink flowers, so the flower can tone into different colour schemes if required. It is a striking addition to any celebration cake.

Latin name: Alstroemeriaceae
Place of origin: South America
Season: Summer
Colours: Orange-yellow and salmon pink
Cakes: Wedding, Birthday, Anniversary

1 Mould a small paste ball. Insert moistened hooked 33 gauge wire to form centre stamen. Leave to dry for 24 hours. Dip in egg white and coat with brown coloured semolina.

2 Fix small cone of paste onto moistened hooked 33 gauge wire. Make 5 stamens. Leave to dry for 24 hours. Coat as for centre stamen.

3 Tape the stamens onto 26 gauge wire. The rounded centre stamen should protrude slightly higher than rest.

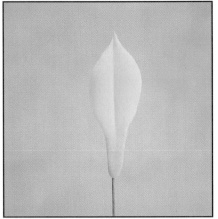

4 Roll out paste leaving slight thickness at base. Using cutter shape **A**, cut petal. Vein centre, smooth and shape. Fix on 28 gauge wire. Make 3 petals.

5 Leave to dry 24 hours. Then dust tip and base with green, and main part with pink. Paint on brown markings.

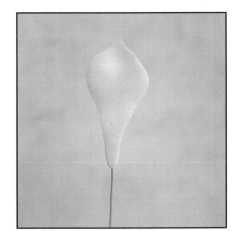

6 Using the same method as step **4**, cut 3 petals with cutter shape **B**. Smooth and shape. Fix on 28 gauge wire. Leave to dry 24 hours.

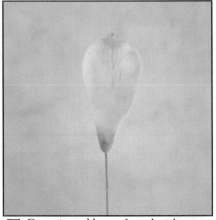

7 Dust tip and base of petal with green. Paint fine green lines at top of petal. Very lightly dust rest of petal with pink.

8 Tape first **A** petal to wire stem.

9 Tape second **A** petal, placing it slightly behind the first.

10 *Tape third **A** petal opposite the other two petals.*

11 *Add first of **B** petals immediately behind first two petals. Tape second and third **B** petals on either side.*

12 *Make and vein a leaf as shown (see p. 12). Fix on 28 gauge wire.*

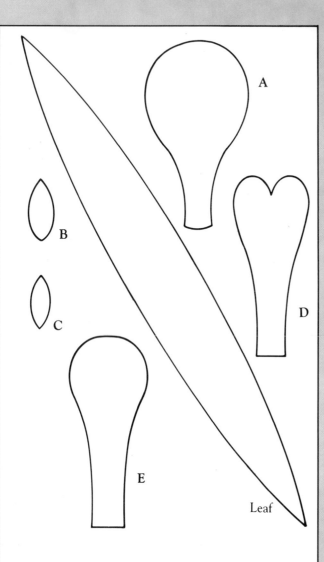

A

B

C

D

E

Leaf

IN Greek mythology Iris was the goddess of the rainbow which served as her bridge between the world of the gods and the earth. One of her tasks was to carry messages of love to mortals whom the gods favoured.

The Iris is a very ancient flower, it is depicted on an Egyptian carving over four thousand years old. It is well known as the emblem of France, the Fleur-de-lis, which was adopted by Louis VII in the twelfth century.

Latin name: Iris Xiphium
Place of origin: Cultivated variety introduced into England from Spain in 1596
Season: Spring/Early Summer
Colours: Blue, yellow, pink and white
Cakes: Birthday, Anniversary
Language of Flowers: Faith, wisdom and valour
Emblem: France

1 Roll out and cut 3 petals from paste, using cutter shape **A**. Ensure the stem of each petal is thicker than the main part. Cover with thin plastic.

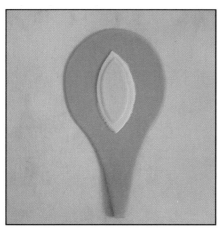

2 Roll out and cut 2 ovals, using cutter shapes **B** and **C**, for each petal. Moisten and fix to centre of petals, as shown.

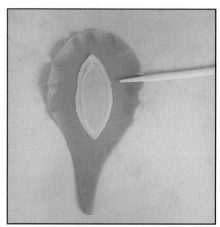

3 Gently frill the edge of one petal, using a cocktail stick (see p. 11).

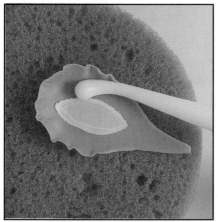

4 Place onto a household sponge and smooth in the oval pieces, using a bone-shaped tool.

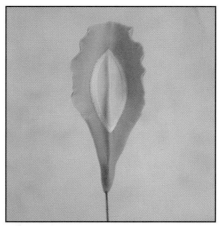

5 Pinch along the centre line to form a pronounced vein. Moisten and insert 30 gauge wire, as shown. Repeat steps *3-5* for remaining petals. Leave to dry 24 hours.

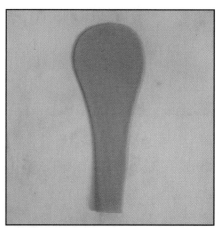

6 Roll out and cut 3 petals, using cutter shape **E**. Ensure the stem of each petal is thicker than the main part. Cover with thin plastic.

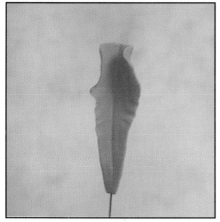

7 Slightly frill and vein each petal using a cocktail stick. Moisten and insert 33 gauge wire into base of each petal. Leave to dry for 24 hours.

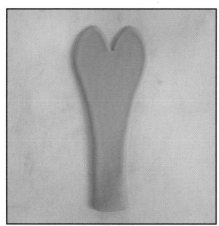

8 Roll out and cut 3 petals, using cutter shape **D**. Cover with thin plastic.

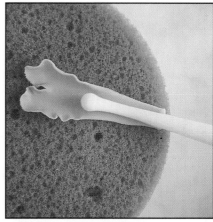

9 Frill edge and, using a bone tool, curl the petal, as shown.

10 Moisten and fix the **D** petal to the **A** petal. Leave to dry for 24 hours.

11 Tape the wires of the **E** petals together to form a circle.

12 Tape the **D** and **A** petals below the **E** petals to complete the flower head. Make and wire leaves as required (see p. 12).

Orange Lily

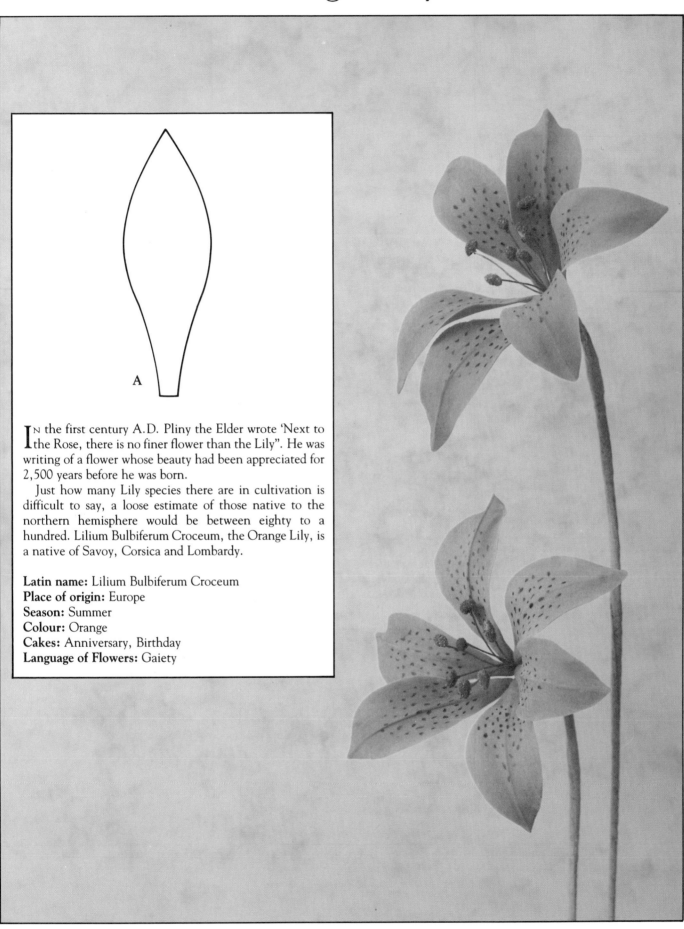

A

I<small>N</small> the first century A.D. Pliny the Elder wrote 'Next to the Rose, there is no finer flower than the Lily". He was writing of a flower whose beauty had been appreciated for 2,500 years before he was born.

Just how many Lily species there are in cultivation is difficult to say, a loose estimate of those native to the northern hemisphere would be between eighty to a hundred. Lilium Bulbiferum Croceum, the Orange Lily, is a native of Savoy, Corsica and Lombardy.

Latin name: Lilium Bulbiferum Croceum
Place of origin: Europe
Season: Summer
Colour: Orange
Cakes: Anniversary, Birthday
Language of Flowers: Gaiety

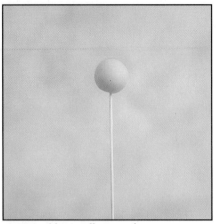

1 Mould a small piece of paste into a ball. Moisten hooked 33 gauge wire and insert into centre of ball, to form a round stamen. Leave to dry for 24 hours.

2 Moisten the stamen and dip it into a mixture of brown confectioners' dusting powder and semolina. Leave to dry for 24 hours.

3 Mould a small piece of paste into an oval shape. Moisten hooked 33 gauge wire and insert into centre of oval to form stamen (6 stamens required). Leave to dry 24 hours.

4 Moisten and dip each oval into the brown mixture. Leave to dry for 24 hours.

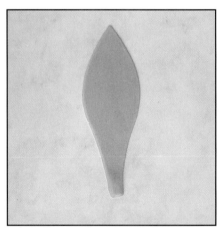

5 Roll out and cut 6 petals from paste, using cutter shape **A**. Ensure the base of each petal is thicker than the main part. Cover with thin plastic.

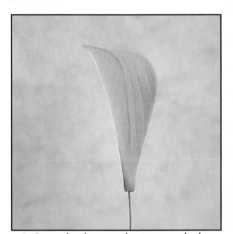

6 Smooth, shape and vein a petal, then moisten and insert 26 gauge wire into the base. Repeat for remaining petals. Leave to dry for 24 hours.

7 Carefully paint and brush each petal, with edible food colouring and confectioners' dusting powder, to the design shown.

8 Paint the stamen wires. Leave to dry then tape the stamens to 24 gauge wire to form the main stem, as shown.

9 Tape a petal to the main stem, positioning the base of the petal to the top of the stem join.

10 Position and tape a second petal.

11 Position and tape a third petal, then fan out, as shown.

12 Carefully tape the remaining petals to the main stem, to complete the flower.

Cattleya Orchid

A   B   C

INTRODUCED into England in 1818, the exotic Cattleya takes its name from William Cattley, a keen North London amateur orchid grower of the early nineteenth century. When he died in 1832, his collection was sold to a specialist firm of nurserymen who propagated them with great success.

The Cattleya is one of the most flamboyant of the Orchid family and it is extremely popular with florists for sprays and bouquets. There are now some sixty species available in many striking colours.

Latin name: Epiphytic or Lithophytic
Place of origin: Central and South America
Season: Summer
Colours: All
Cakes: Wedding, Anniversary, Valentine
Language of Flowers: Magnificence

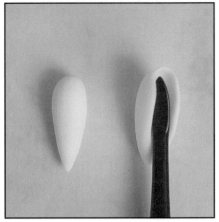

1 Hollow out a moulded paste cone with a modelling tool to form the throat. Moisten and insert hooked 24 gauge wire. Leave to dry for 24 hours.

2 With a clean, dry and fine artists' brush, tint the inside of the throat with confectioners' dusting powder. Paint brown spots as shown.

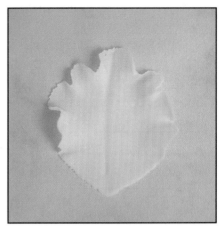

3 Using cutter shape **A** cut a large petal. Using a cocktail stick, well frill the edges and vein down the centre.

4 Moisten base of petal and fold around throat as shown. Leave to dry for 24 hours.

5 Using cutter shape **B** cut a petal. Ensure paste is thicker at base. Lightly smooth edges. Vein the centre and then turn petal over. Moisten and insert 33 gauge wire.

6 Leave petal to dry on a curved shape, vein uppermost. Leave to dry for 24 hours (2 petals required).

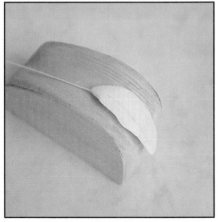

7 Using cutter shape **C** cut a petal. Lightly smooth the edges. Vein the centre and insert moistened 33 gauge wire. Dry vein down on a curved surface for 24 hours.

8 Using cutter shape **C** cut a petal and very lightly smooth edges. Vein and insert moistened 33 gauge wire. Dry vein up on a curved surface for 24 hours (2 required).

9 Brush the outside top of the throat and the spots on the large petal as shown.

10 Tape the two **B** shape petals above the large petal and throat.

11 Tape the narrow petal from step *7* at the top behind the flower.

12 Tape the narrow petals from step *8* to the left and right of the large petal as shown to complete the flower.

Fuchsia

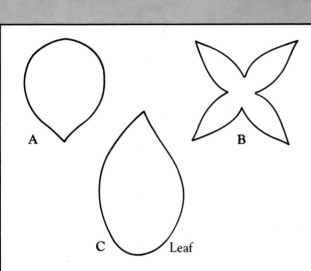

A

B

C   Leaf

The Fuchsias do not have a very well documented early history, but the Royal Gardens at Kew had a plant of Fuchsia Coccinea in one of the greenhouses in the eighteenth century. It is recorded in the Botanical Magazine 1789 that a Captain Firth brought back a plant from Brazil and presented it to them.

The generic name Fuchsia had been coined nearly one hundred years earlier by Père Charles Plummier. He discovered the plant in the Dominican Republic. The name Fuchsia was a compliment to Leonhart Fuchs, a Doctor of Medicine and a very able botanist.

During the nineteenth century, Fuchsia cultivation reached a very high standard but World War I brought big changes and gardens were especially hard hit. The Fuchsia declined in popularity but it has enjoyed a revival with Fuchsia Clubs flourishing everywhere.

Latin name: Fuchsia Triphylla
Place of origin: South America
Season: Spring and Summer
Colours: Various with a predominance of reds, pinks and purples
Cakes: Wedding, Birthday, Anniversary, Engagement
Language of Flowers: Good taste

TO MAKE AN OPEN FLOWER

1 Tape 7 short red stamens and 1 long yellow stamen to a length of 26 gauge wire.

2 Moisten and fix a small amount of paste round the join, as shown.

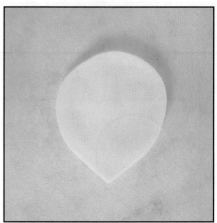

3 Roll out and cut 4 petals from paste, using cutter shape A. Cover with thin plastic.

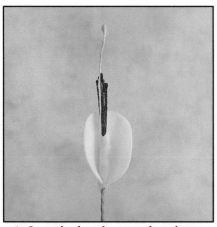

4 Smooth edge of one petal, and press it in the centre to form a shallow dish shape. Moisten and fix it around the stem in the position shown.

5 Smooth and shape another petal and fix to one side of the first petal.

6 Smooth and shape remaining petals and fix to one side of the previous petal. Tuck edge of last petal towards centre of flower, as shown.

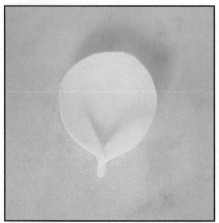

7 Roll out and cut 6 petals, using cutter shape A. Smooth and shape each petal into a dish shape, then pinch together the base of each petal, as shown.

8 Moisten and fix the petals around the flower, overlapping to form a tight bloom.

9 Paint the base of the flower with edible food colouring.

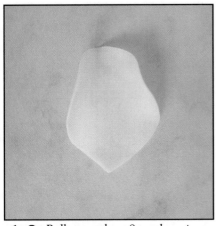

10 Roll out and cut 8 petals, using cutter shape **A**. Cover with thin plastic. Smooth and shape 2 petals as shown. Moisten and fix to the flower. Colour as in step **9**.

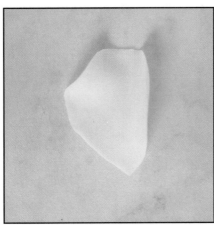

11 Smooth and shape a further 2 petals as shown. Moisten and fix to the flower. Colour as in step **9**.

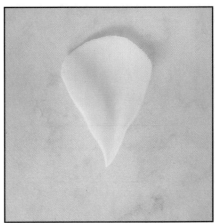

12 Smooth and shape remaining 4 petals to shape shown. Moisten and fix to the flower. Colour as in step **9**.

13 Picture shows the flower with open petals around outside. Leave to dry for 24 hours.

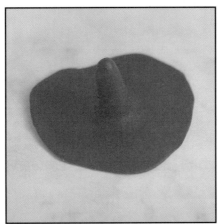

14 Make and shape a paste cone, using a strong colour. Roll out base of cone.

15 Cut out the calyx, using cutter shape **B**. Smooth and curl up each petal using a bone-shaped modelling tool.

16 Moisten stem at base of flower and insert into the calyx. Fix tightly to the flower as shown.

17 Mould a seed pod and fix to base of calyx. Leave to dry for 24 hours.

18 Roll out, cut, shape and vein leaves, using cutter shape **C**, ensuring base of leaf is thicker. Fix to 26 gauge wire. Leave to dry for 24 hours. Colour as required.

TO MAKE A BUD

19 Mould a piece of paste into a triangular shaped bud. Moisten and insert hooked shaped wire into centre.

20 Mould paste, moisten and fix to base of bud, as shown.

21 Mould and shape a further piece of paste to form a seed pod. Moisten and fix to base to complete the bud. Leave to dry for 24 hours.

Buttercup

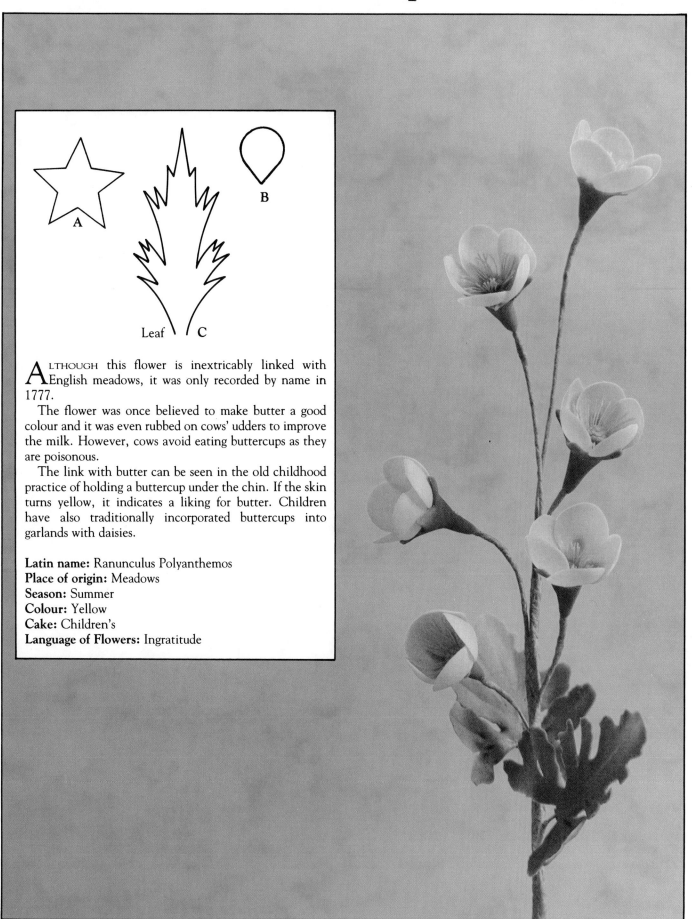

A B

Leaf C

ALTHOUGH this flower is inextricably linked with English meadows, it was only recorded by name in 1777.

The flower was once believed to make butter a good colour and it was even rubbed on cows' udders to improve the milk. However, cows avoid eating buttercups as they are poisonous.

The link with butter can be seen in the old childhood practice of holding a buttercup under the chin. If the skin turns yellow, it indicates a liking for butter. Children have also traditionally incorporated buttercups into garlands with daisies.

Latin name: Ranunculus Polyanthemos
Place of origin: Meadows
Season: Summer
Colour: Yellow
Cake: Children's
Language of Flowers: Ingratitude

1 Wind fine yellow cotton round two fingers several times. Remove, and twist into a figure of eight.

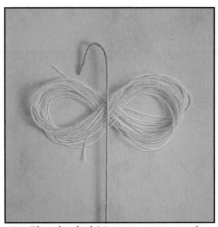

2 Place hooked 26 gauge wire over the centre of the loops and twist the hook.

3 Tape the join and then carefully trim the ends.

*4 Mould a cone and roll out the edges. Using cutter shape **A** carefully cut a calyx. Smooth cut edges with a bone-shaped tool.*

5 Immediately insert wire stem through calyx centre. Moisten join and pull stem through until join is hidden. Leave to dry for 24 hours.

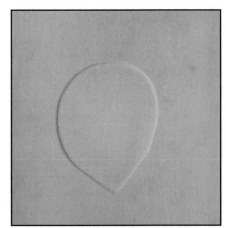

*6 Using cutter shape **B** cut 5 petals. Cover with thin plastic.*

7 Gently smooth the petal edges with a bone-shaped tool and hollow the centre.

8 Moisten and fix petal base onto the calyx.

9 Moisten and fix the remaining 4 petals, overlapping as shown. Leave to dry for 24 hours.

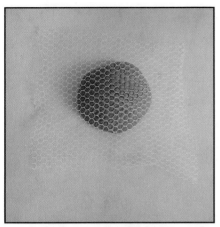

10 Make a small ball of green paste. Press fine net onto the ball to texture. Carefully remove the net.

11 Moisten ball and place in the centre of the stamens.

12 Using cutter shape **C**, make, vein and wire a leaf. Leave to dry for 24 hours.

Honeysuckle

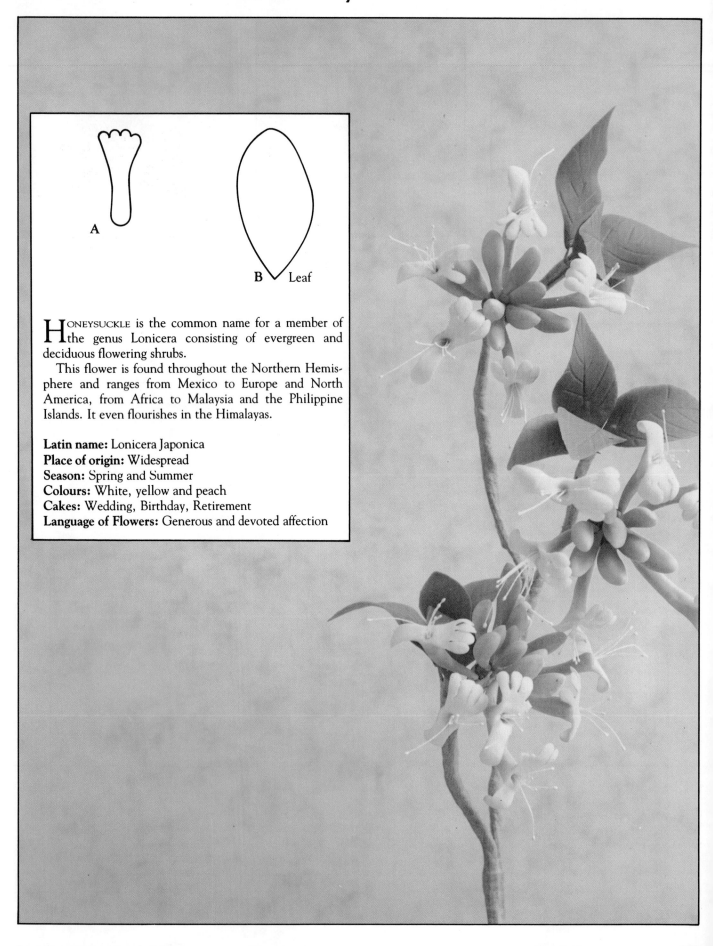

A

B Leaf

Honeysuckle is the common name for a member of the genus Lonicera consisting of evergreen and deciduous flowering shrubs.

This flower is found throughout the Northern Hemisphere and ranges from Mexico to Europe and North America, from Africa to Malaysia and the Philippine Islands. It even flourishes in the Himalayas.

Latin name: Lonicera Japonica
Place of origin: Widespread
Season: Spring and Summer
Colours: White, yellow and peach
Cakes: Wedding, Birthday, Retirement
Language of Flowers: Generous and devoted affection

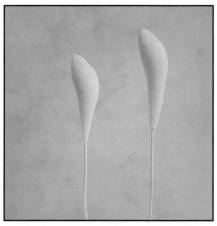

1 Make an elongated paste ball and insert hooked, moistened 33 gauge wire to form a bud (6 large and 6 small buds required). Leave to dry for 24 hours.

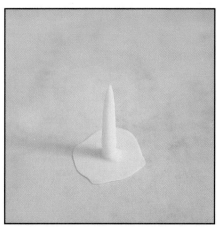

2 Mould a tall cone and roll out the edges. Elongate centre into a tall pillar as shown.

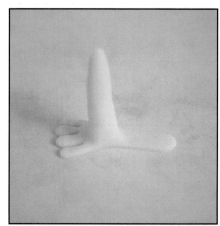

3 Carefully cut base to shape shown using cutter shape **A**.

4 Gently thin petal edges and curve as shown. Elongate and bend the pillar as shown. Using a cocktail stick, make a hole in the centre.

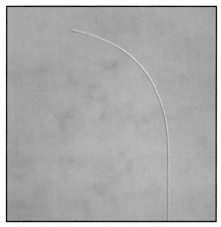

5 Bend a length of 30 gauge wire as shown.

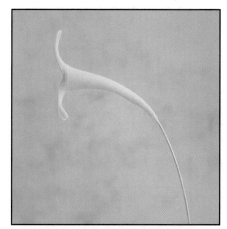

6 Moisten and carefully insert curved wire following curvature of flower head (7 flowers required).

7 Insert 1 long and 4 short stamen wires into the flower centre. Bend to shape as shown. Leave to dry for 24 hours.

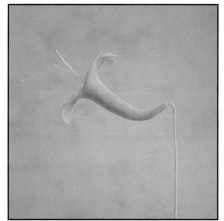

8 Using a clean, fine and dry artists' brush, dust flower with confectioners' dusting powder.

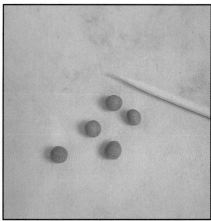

9 Form very small balls of paste to represent seed pods. Leave to dry for 24 hours.

10 Dust the small buds from step **1** with confectioners' dusting powder. Tape together to form centre of flower.

11 Dust the large buds from step **1** with confectioners' dusting powder. Tape the buds around flower centre. Fix seed pods from step **9** at base as shown.

12 Tape flowers to outside of flower centre. Fix further small seed pods to base of flowers. Using cutter shape **B** cut, shape, vein and wire leaves (see p. 12).

Poor Man's Orchid

A B

THERE are over one thousand of the Epidendrum species to which the Poor Man's Orchid belongs.

These small orchids bloom in several colours, which makes them extremely useful for colour co-ordinated cakes and table decorations. In their native habitat many of them bloom throughout most of the year. Indeed, it is recorded that one plant flowered continuously for four years.

Latin name: Schizamthus
Place of origin: Central and South America
Season: Summer (in England)
Colours: Pale pink, mauve, yellow, red and orange
Cake: Wedding

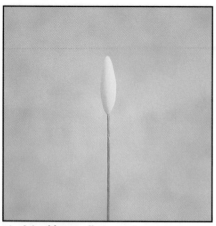

1 Mould a small piece of paste into a cone. Moisten 28 gauge wire (without hook) and insert into centre of ball. Leave to dry for 24 hours.

2 Using cutter shape **A** roll out and cut a petal.

3 Carefully make 3 cuts in the end of each of the straight sided shapes.

4 Frill all the edges of the petal with a cocktail stick (see p.11).

5 Moisten the base of the petal and wrap around the flower centre. Leave to dry for 24 hours.

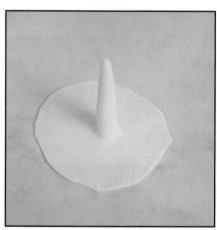

6 Mould a cone and roll out the base (the cone needs to be 1cm (½") high when finished).

7 Using cutter shape **B** carefully cut out the shape shown.

8 Ball and shape 4 petals to curve downwards. Ball and shape the fifth petal to curve upwards. Using a cocktail stick, make a hole in the centre of cone.

9 Moisten centre of cone and insert wire stem carefully placing the centre petals in position. Mould the cone down the wire. Leave to dry for 24 hours.

10 Using edible food colouring and a fine brush, paint 6 deep pink spots around the base of the top petal.

11 Dust the edges of all the petals with pink confectioners' dusting powder.

12 Dust the cone pink and then dust green colouring at the base of the cone.

Autumn

THE colours of autumn can be both subtle and vibrant with rich shades of purple and reds, or earthy browns fading through glowing orange to gold and palest yellow. Autumn is the season of mellow fruitfulness and the luscious fruits of autumn provide the cake-decorator with an unusual focus for a seasonal celebration cake, as can be seen in the cake illustrated here which combines Blackberries with autumn fungi.

This season offers the floral artist an unrivalled opportunity to experiment with colour and texture. The vibrant Poppy could be used to create a most unusual Harvest Festival cake while the exotic Lilies and Orchids offers delicate and unusual colourings for celebration cakes.

SEASONAL FLOWERS

Month	September	October	November
English	Morning Glory	Hop	Chrysanthemum
Japanese	Chrysanthemum	Nanukusa	Maple
Chinese	Mallow	Chrysanthemum	Gardenia

SEASONAL COLOURS

September   *Silver*
October   *Pale Blue*
November   *Deep Red*

FESTIVALS

Harvest Thanksgiving
Michaelmas   *29th September*
Hallowe'en   *31st October*
Thanksgiving   *November*
Bonfire Night   *5th November*
Remembrance Day   *11th November*
St. Andrew's Day   *30th November*

September
1 Orpine
2 Golden Rod
3 Common Fleabane
4 Pink Soapwort
5 Mushroom
6 Dandelion
7 Golden Starwort
8 Blue Starwort
9 Golden Rod
10 Autumn Crocus
11 Meadow Saffron
12 Passion Flower
13 Crocus
14 Passion Flower
15 Byzantine Saffrona
16 Sea-blue Starwort
17 Mallow
18 Pendulous Starwort
19 Devil's-bite Scabious
20 Meadow Saffron
21 Passion Flower
22 Boletus-tree
23 White Starwort

24 Fungus
25 Great Boletus
26 Golden Rod
27 White Starwort
28 Golden Rod
29 Michaelmas Daisy
30 Golden Amaryllis

October
1 Lowly Amaryllis
2 Soapwort
3 Downy Helenium
4 Southernwood
5 Chamomile
6 Feverfew
7 Chrysanthemum
8 Sweet Maudlin
9 Milky Mushroom
10 Cape Aletris
11 Common Holly
12 Wavy Fleabane
13 Yellow Helenium
14 Indian Fleabane
15 Sweet Sultan

16 Yarrow
17 Dwarf Sunflower
18 Mushroom
19 Thickseed
20 Sweet Sultan
21 Silphium
22 Starwort
23 Silphium
24 Starwort
25 Fleabane
26 Golden Rod
27 Starwort
28 Chrysanthemum
29 Narcissus
30 Mixen Mushroom
31 Thickseed

November
1 Laurustinus
2 Winter Cherry
3 Primrose
4 Arbutus
5 Winter Cherry
6 Yew

7 Furcroa
8 Cape Aletris
9 Aletris
10 Scots Fir
11 Weymouth Pine
12 Aloe
13 Bay
14 Portuguese Laurel
15 Coltsfoot
16 African Hemp
17 Thorn Apple
18 Passion Flower
19 Passion Flower
20 Stapelia
21 Wood Sorrel
22 Wood Sorrel
23 Sorrel
24 Stapelia
25 Sweet Butterbur
26 Sorrel
27 Sorrel
28 Stapelia
29 Sphenogyne
30 Sorrel

ALTHOUGH white filler blossom is illustrated, each season has its own particular colours and shapes. The delicate blossoms are extremely useful when making up sprays for both cake and table decorations.

Many different effects can be achieved simply and easily by colouring the petals in different ways. By dusting the tips of the petals delicately, a halo of colour can be created, whilst an illusion of depth can be given to the flower by colouring its centre. Lustre colours are available in gold and silver as well as several soft-hued shades, and they give a gentle sheen to the flower which is particularly attractive when used on wedding anniversary cakes.

Petals can also be shaped from several shades of paste and arranged appropriately on the stems. Inserting coloured stamens into a white blossom can quickly transform a flower. For instance, a purple stamen creates a striking effect which can be heightened by tinting the flower centre in a lighter shade.

Different effects can also be achieved by altering the shape and angle of the flowers. Petals can be round or sharp, small or large; flowers flat or bell-shaped, open or closed. Stems can be varied by using different gauges of wire. They can be long and delicate, a thin stem being formed by winding tape at a steep angle, or thick and chunky by winding the tape almost horizontally. The blossoms can be clustered together or spread out along the stem.

The overall effect of the finished arrangement should be carefully planned before commencing work, giving particular attention to the placing of the flowers specific to the occasion, and the main flowers should always be made first. The overall shape may require several different sizes and lengths of filler blossom sprays.

When copying a bridal bouquet, the fill-in flowers can be adapted, from the instructions given here, to match the shape and colour of the bouquet.

The wedding cake illustrated on page 43 gives a magnificent example of the way in which delicate filler blossom can be used to contrast with large, dominant flowers.

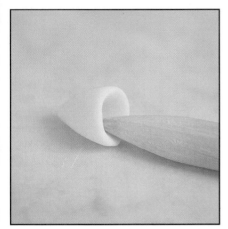

1 Make a small cone from paste and hollow out the centre with a cocktail stick.

2 Make 5 cuts evenly around the circumference. Pinch the end of each petal. Flatten and shape by placing the thumb on top, and the finger underneath, the petal.

3 Vein petal centres with a cocktail stick and pinch to a point. Insert moistened 30 gauge wire into cone. Moisten and insert stamen. Tape blossoms to 26 gauge wire.

Kaffir Lily

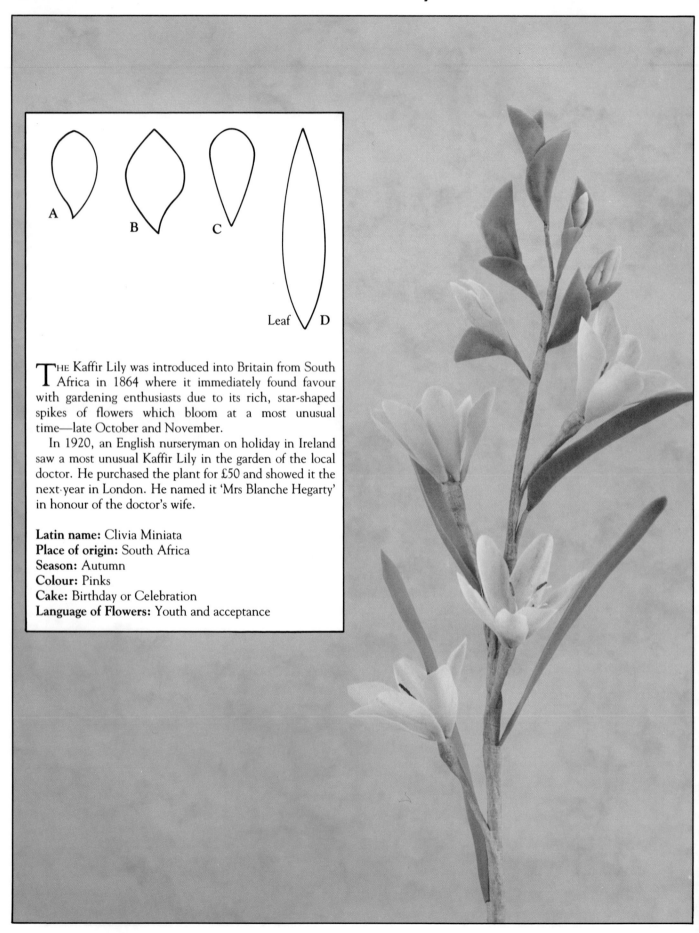

A   B   C

Leaf   D

THE Kaffir Lily was introduced into Britain from South Africa in 1864 where it immediately found favour with gardening enthusiasts due to its rich, star-shaped spikes of flowers which bloom at a most unusual time—late October and November.

In 1920, an English nurseryman on holiday in Ireland saw a most unusual Kaffir Lily in the garden of the local doctor. He purchased the plant for £50 and showed it the next year in London. He named it 'Mrs Blanche Hegarty' in honour of the doctor's wife.

Latin name: Clivia Miniata
Place of origin: South Africa
Season: Autumn
Colour: Pinks
Cake: Birthday or Celebration
Language of Flowers: Youth and acceptance

TO MAKE LEAF BUDS

1 Make a small cone of paste and fix onto moistened, hooked 26 gauge wire to form a bud.

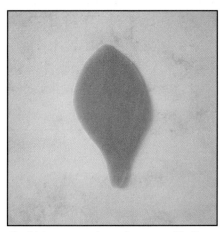

*2 Using cutter shape **A**, cut and ball a leaf.*

3 Moisten leaf and fold around bud.

*4 Using cutter shape **B**, cut a second leaf, moisten and lace opposite the **A** leaf as shown.*

*5 Cut a second **B** leaf, moisten and place below the first on the opposite side as shown. Leave to dry for 24 hours.*

TO MAKE A FLOWER BUD

6 Mould a small cone of paste and insert moistened, hooked 26 gauge wire to form a flower bud.

7 Using a cocktail stick, carefully mark 6 indentations to simulate petals.

*8 Using cutter shape **B**, cut and ball a leaf. Moisten and fold around flower bud as shown. Leave to dry for 24 hours.*

TO MAKE A HALF-OPEN BUD

9 Mould a slightly larger cone of pink paste and fix on 26 gauge wire. Make 6 cuts in the paste and pull slightly open.

10 *Twist petals around as shown leaving top slightly open.*

11 *Using cutter shape **B**, cut and ball a leaf. Moisten and fix below the bud.*

12 *Using cutter shape **A**, cut and ball a leaf. Moisten and fix below the larger leaf. Leave to dry or 24 hours.*

TO MAKE A HALF-OPEN FLOWER

13 *Colour the tips of 3 thick stamens. Tape with 3 thin stamens to the top of 26 gauge wire.*

14 *Make a cone of paste and cut 6 petals. Thin petals and shape slightly. Insert moistened wire stem through centre and position stamens carefully.*

15 *Using cutter shape **B**, cut and ball a leaf. Moisten and fix below the petals.*

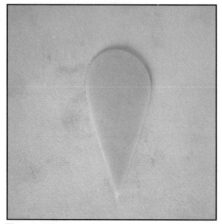

TO MAKE A FLOWER

16 *Roll out paste leaving the bottom slightly thicker. Using cutter shape **C**, cut a petal (6 petals required). Cover with thin plastic.*

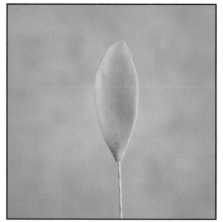

17 *Ball, shape and vein the petal. Insert moistened 30 gauge wire into base of petal. Leave to dry for 24 hours. Dust with confectioners' dusting powder.*

18 *Repeat step **13** to make stem. Evenly space 3 petals around the stem and tape into place.*

19 Tape 3 more petals onto the flower, placing them between the petals in the first layer.

TO MAKE A FLOWER SPRAY
20 Tape leaf and flower buds into a spray with the leaf bud at the top. Add half-open flower and then fully opened flower beneath.

21 Using cutter shape **D**, make, vein and wire a leaf (see p. 12) and tape into position below the flowers (see flower spray in illustration below).

KAFFIR LILY

Poppy

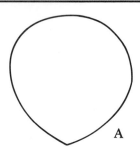

A

THE Poppy used to be a familiar sight in English cornfields and it is one of the most ancient of plants. Legend has it that it was essential to the health of wheat. The Greek goddess Demeter cultivated it amongst her golden wheat. The Romans called this goddess Ceres, origin of the word cereal.

In ancient times, the Poppy was the emblem of sleep, rest and repose. The god Morpheus was said to fashion crowns of Poppies for those to whom he gave the gift of sleep. In Egypt dried Poppies have been found in tombs over three thousand years old, where they formed part of the rites to ensure eternal life.

In the present day Poppies have become the emblem of remembrance. During the First World War Poppies grew in abundance on the shell-torn fields of Flanders and it was adopted in remembrance of those killed in battle.

The beautifully coloured cultivated Poppies grown today are all from the seed of one variegated Poppy found in a vicarage garden a hundred years ago. The Rev. William Wilks painstakingly propagated the seed and created a whole range of new colours.

Latin name: Papaveraceae
Place of origin: The Middle East
Season: Summer/Autumn
Colours: Mainly red, white and pink
Cake: Harvest Festival
Language of Flowers: Remembrance and consolation
Emblem: British Legion

1 Make a cone of green paste and flatten the top. Insert moistened hooked 26 gauge wire.

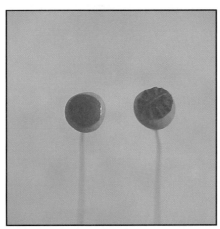

2 Make a disc of darker paste, moisten and attach to top of Poppy head. Mark top of disc with lines as shown.

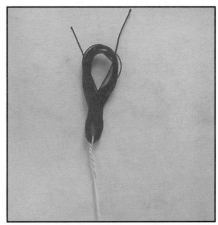

3 Loop black cotton several times round two fingers. Remove and twist as shown. Place hooked 33 gauge wire through bottom loop and twist to secure (4 required).

4 Trim cotton loops and place around the Poppy head. Tape into place.

5 Using cutter shape **A**, cut 4 petals ensuring that the base is slightly thicker. Cover with thin plastic.

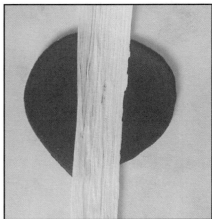

6 Shape with a bone-shaped tool and vein the petal lightly.

7 Slightly frill the edge of the petal with a cocktail stick (see p.11).

8 Moisten and insert 33 gauge wire in the base of the petal. Leave 2 inside petals to dry for 24 hours in a shallow dish as shown.

9 Leave 2 outside petals to dry for 24 hours as shown with the edge of the petals over the dish edge.

10 *Tape an inside petal to the Poppy head.*

11 *Tape the other inside petal opposite the first.*

12 *Tape the 2 outside petals as shown to complete the flower.* **Note:** *Buds can be formed from wired cones of paste marked to simulate petals.*

Rubrum Lily

A

THIS flower is another of the Lily species. An extremely hardy plant, it is found in Bhutan and Nepal on the slopes of the Himalayas.

As the flower blooms on into late autumn it is extremely useful for decorating wedding and anniversary cakes and for providing attractive table decorations at a time when fresh blooms are not always available.

Latin name: Lilium Sherriffiac (Rubrum)
Place of origin: Bhutan and Nepal
Season: Summer and Autumn
Colour: Pink
Cakes: Wedding, Anniversary, Birthday
Language of Flowers: Coquetry

1 Make an elongated paste ball and insert hooked, moistened 33 gauge white wire (6 required). Make a further ball and insert hooked moistened 33 gauge green wire.

2 Leave to dry for 24 hours. Moisten with egg white and then dip in coloured semolina. Leave to dry for 24 hours.

3 Tape together onto 26 gauge wire with the round stamen protruding above the rest.

*4 Using cutter shape **A** cut a petal, ensure paste is thicker at base. Insert moistened 33 gauge wire.*

5 Place petal on a clean, dry household sponge and shape with a bone-shaped modelling tool.

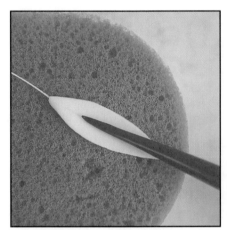

6 Vein centre and fold in half. Immediately unfold to create a deep centre groove.

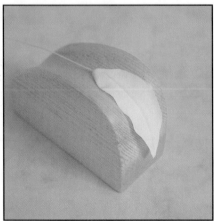

7 Leave petals to dry on a curved surface for 24 hours (6 required).

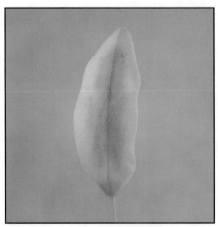

8 Delicately dust with petal dust using a clean, fine, dry artists' brush.

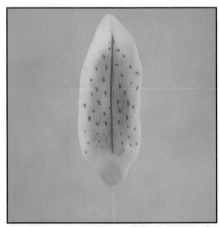

9 Paint centre vein and dots over petal as shown using liquid edible food colouring.

10 *Tape the first petal below the stamen then bend the wire to the shape shown.*

11 *Add the second and third petals above and to the left and right of the first.*

12 *Add the remaining petals behind the first row, positioned between the petals as shown.*

Blackberry

THE Blackberry has been a feature of the English hedgerow for centuries and there are over forty species. It was much prized in olden times for making jams and jellies. A warming wine was also made which was a tonic, as well as a pleasure to drink, as it contained a large amount of iron.

Blackberrying was an important country pursuit and children would be sent out into the fields to gather the precious berries, arriving home with a brightly coloured mouth as evidence of how much they had enjoyed the berries straight off the bushes.

Latin name: Rubus Fruiticosus
Place of origin: Rocky banks and wasteland
Season: Autumn
Colours: White flower, red/black fruit
Cakes: Autumn, Birthday, Harvest Festival, Retirement
Language of Flowers: Envy

TO MAKE A FLOWER

1 Wind cotton round 2 fingers several times. Cut in half and secure with 26 gauge wire, then tape the join. Dust the ends of the cotton as shown.

*2 Mould a cone and roll out the edges. Using cutter shape **A** carefully cut a calyx. Smooth cut edges with a bone-shaped tool.*

3 Immediately insert wire stem through calyx centre. Moisten join and pull stem through until join is hidden. Leave to dry for 24 hours.

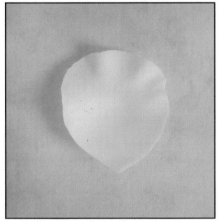

*4 Using cutter shape **B**, cut and ball the upper edge of a petal as shown (5 petals required).*

5 Moisten and fix each petal base onto the calyx, overlapping as shown.

TO MAKE A BERRY

6 Make a paste ball, moisten and insert a hooked length of 26 gauge wire.

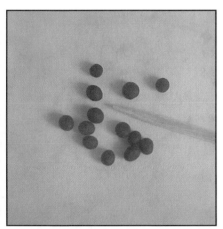

7 Make plenty of tiny balls to represent the seeds.

8 Moisten seeds and fix to the large ball, beginning at the top and covering closely.

9 Completely cover the ball and leave to dry for 24 hours. Lightly varnish with confectioners' varnish.

10 *Using cutter shape **C** cut a calyx. Moisten and insert wire stem through centre. Fix into place at base of berry.*

11 *Using cutter shape **D**, cut and vein a leaf, ensure base is thicker. Moisten and insert 33 gauge wire stem. Leave to dry 24 for hours.*

12 *Lightly varnish the leaf. Tape to form a spray as shown below.*

Cymbidium Orchid

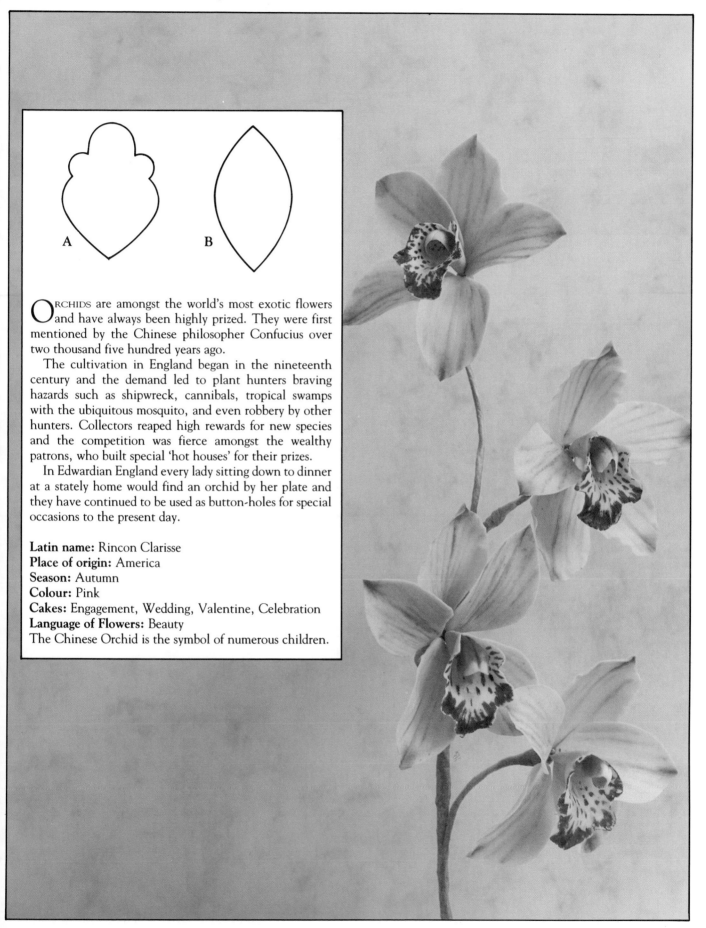

ORCHIDS are amongst the world's most exotic flowers and have always been highly prized. They were first mentioned by the Chinese philosopher Confucius over two thousand five hundred years ago.

The cultivation in England began in the nineteenth century and the demand led to plant hunters braving hazards such as shipwreck, cannibals, tropical swamps with the ubiquitous mosquito, and even robbery by other hunters. Collectors reaped high rewards for new species and the competition was fierce amongst the wealthy patrons, who built special 'hot houses' for their prizes.

In Edwardian England every lady sitting down to dinner at a stately home would find an orchid by her plate and they have continued to be used as button-holes for special occasions to the present day.

Latin name: Rincon Clarisse
Place of origin: America
Season: Autumn
Colour: Pink
Cakes: Engagement, Wedding, Valentine, Celebration
Language of Flowers: Beauty
The Chinese Orchid is the symbol of numerous children.

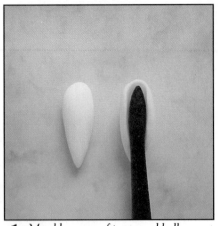

1 Mould a cone of paste and hollow out the centre as shown to form the throat of the flower.

2 Insert moistened 26 gauge wire and leave to dry 24 hours. With edible food colouring and a fine brush, paint marks on the throat as shown.

3 Dust the outside of the throat using confectioners' dusting powder.

4 Using cutter shape **A**, roll out and cut the throat petal.

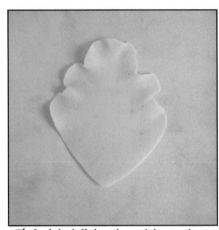

5 Lightly frill the edges of the petal using a cocktail stick (see p.11).

6 Moisten throat petal and fold around the throat as shown. Insert 2 yellow pollen strands. Leave to dry for 24 hours.

7 Carefully colour the completed throat as shown.

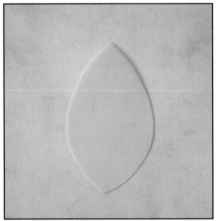

8 Using cutter shape **B**, roll out and cut a petal with slight thickness at the base.

9 Shape the petal with a bone-shaped tool and frill the edges lightly. Vein and insert 26 gauge wire into base of the petal. Leave to dry 24 hours. Colour tip and veins.

10 Repeat steps *8-9* but leave to dry over a curved surface so that the petal turns slightly outward (*4 petals required*).

11 Tape 2 outward facing petals from step *10* above the throat, as shown.

12 Tape petal from step *9* behind the throat and then add the remaining 2 petals below the throat.

Winter

During the dark days of Winter the Pansy provides a welcome splash of colour for use on celebration cakes and the brilliant flame-like Poinsettia is a striking addition to a Christmas Cake, blending well with seasonal Holly and Mistletoe. The cake-decorator also has the opportunity of using the gentler colours of the winter blooms such as the Christmas Rose, used here for a Christmas Cake, and the delicate bell-like Snowdrop.
Sugar flowers are also ideal for replacing expensive cut flowers at this time of year, creating a striking centre piece for the festive table or an unusual place setting for that special occasion.

Seasonal Flowers

Month	December	January	February
English	*Holly*	*Snowdrop*	*Primrose*
Japanese	*Bamboo*	*Pine*	*Plum*
Chinese	*Poppy*	*Plum Blossom*	*Peach Blossom*

Seasonal Colours

December *Purple*
January *Dark Green*
February *Electric Blue*

Festivals

Christmas Eve *24th December*
Christmas Day *25th December*
Boxing Day *26th December*
New Year's Eve *31st December*
Wassail Eve *5th January*
Epiphany *6th January*
Burns Night *25th January*
Carnation Day *29th January*
Candlemas *1st February*
Valentine's Day *14th February*

December
1 Stapelia
2 Lemon Geodurum
3 Indian-tree
4 Gooseberry
5 Hibiscus
6 Heath
7 Hairy Achania
8 Arbor Vitae
9 Corsican Spruce
10 Portugal Cypress
11 Aleppo Pine
12 Ground Heath
13 Arbor Vitae
14 Swamp Pine
15 Pitch Pine
16 Arbor Vitae
17 White Cedar
18 New Holland Cypress
19 Bicolour Heath
20 Stone Pine
21 Sparrow-wort
22 Pellucid Heath
23 Cedar of Lebanon
24 Frankincense Pine
25 Holly
26 Purple Heath
27 Flame Heath
28 Heath
29 Heath
30 Ponthieva
31 Winter Jasmine

January
1 Laurustinus
2 Groundsel
3 Persian Iris
4 Hazel
5 Hellebore
6 Screw Moss
7 Portuguese Laurel
8 Yellow Tremella
9 Laurel
10 Gorse
11 Early Moss
12 Moss
13 Common Yew
14 Barren Strawberry
15 Ivy
16 Red Dead Nettle
17 Garden Anemone
18 Four-toothed Moss
19 White Dead Nettle
20 Woolly Dead Nettle
21 Black Hellebore
22 Whitlow Grass
23 Peziza
24 Stalkless Moss
25 Winter Hellebore
26 Coltsfoot
27 Earth Moss
28 Double Daisy
29 Flowering Fern
30 Spleenwort
31 Hart's-tongue

February
1 Bay Tree
2 Snowdrop
3 Water Moss
4 Goldilocks
5 Primrose
6 Blue Hyacinth
7 Cyclamen
8 Hair Moss
9 Roman Narcissus
10 Mezeron
11 Red Primrose
12 Anemone
13 Polyanthus
14 Yellow Crocus
15 Golden Crocus
16 Lilac Primrose
17 Scotch Crocus
18 Wall Speedwell
19 Field Speedwell
20 Blue-eyes
21 White Crocus
22 Herb Margaret
23 Apricot Blossom
24 Great Fern
25 Peach Blossom
26 Lesser Periwinkle
27 Lungwort
28 Purple Crocus
29 Striped Crocus

A

Fᴵᴸᴸᴇʀ blossom can be varied in colour and shape according to the season and it is very useful when making up sprays for cake and table decorations. When copying a bridal bouquet, the delicate fill-in flowers can be adapted, from the instructions given here, to match the shape and colour of the bouquet.

A simple and easy way to achieve a wide variety of effects is to colour the petals in different ways. Delicately dusting the tips of the petals, as illustrated here, creates a halo of colour, whilst colouring the centre of the flower gives the illusion of greater depth. Lustre colours impart a gentle sheen to the flower and are available in gold and silver as well as several soft-hued shades, and they are particularly useful for wedding anniversary cakes.

Several shades of paste can be used to shape the petals before arranging them appropriately on the stems. Coloured stamens inserted into a white blossom can quickly transform a flower. For example, a purple stamen creates a striking centre and the effect can be heightened by tinting the flower centre in a lighter shade.

Different effects can be created by varying the shape and angle of the flowers. Petals can be round or sharp, large or small; flowers flat or bell-shaped, open or closed. Different gauges of wire can be used to make stems long and delicate or thick and chunky. By winding tape at a steep angle a thin stem is formed, and winding almost horizontally results in a thicker stem. Blossoms can be spread out along the stem or clustered together.

Several different sizes and lengths of filler blossom sprays may be needed to make up the overall shape of the finished arrangement. The effect should be carefully planned before commencing work, giving particular attention to the placing of flowers specific to the occasion. The main flowers should always be made first.

The wedding cake illustrated on page 43 gives a beautiful example of how delicate filler blossoms can provide an attractive contrast when combined with large, dominant flowers.

1 Make a cone from paste. Flatten out the base as shown using a small rolling pin.

2 Using cutter shape **A**, carefully place over the cone and cut the base to form petals. Slightly hollow out the centre. Shape petals appropriately.

3 Moisten and insert 26 gauge wire through the cone base. Insert stamen and leave to dry 24 hours. Make several blossoms and tape onto 26 gauge wire to form sprigs.

Hazelnut

A

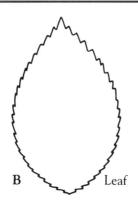

B   Leaf

Tʜᴇ Hazel was regarded by the Celts as the Tree of Wisdom. Cultivated by the ancient Greeks and Romans, it was attributed with magical power well as providing the wattle for wattle and daub buildings and many ancient Hazel copses still exist.

Nutting parties would go out in the Autumn to gather Hazel nuts and a traditional saying was 'many nuts, many marriages' as this was a time of match making. Victorian lovers were also advised to sit under a Hazel tree if they wished to be reconciled.

Latin name: Corylus Avellana
Place of origin: Britain
Season: Catkins in Spring, Nuts in Autumn
Colour: Catkins — yellow, Nuts — green and brown
Cakes: Birthday, Retirement, Autumn celebrations
Language of Flowers: Reconciliation
Emblem: St. Philibert

1   *Make a cone of pale green paste and shape into nut by flattening sides and top. Moisten hooked 24 gauge wire and insert into cone. Leave to dry for 24 hours. (Side View).*

2   *Front View of the hazelnut showing the width of the nut shape required.*

3   *Dust, as shown, shading the base of nut darker than the top.*

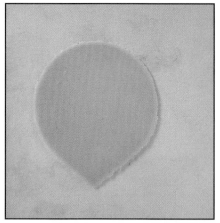

4   *Cut a leaf shape using cutter shape* **A**.

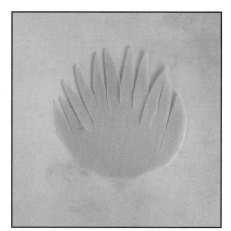

5   *Cut off base of leaf and feather the top, as shown, by making uneven cuts with scissors.*

6   *Moisten bottom half of leaf and fix to one side of nut. Curl leaf as shown.*

7   *Make a second leaf and fix opposite the other. Curl leaf as shown. Leave to dry for 24 hours.*

8   *Dust leaf with deep shade at base, paler towards top.*

9   *Roll out paste, leaving thickness at base and cut leaf using cutter shape* **B**. *Vein and fix onto moistened 26 gauge wire. Leave to dry for 24 hours.*

10 Dust leaf with confectioners' dusting powder as shown.

11 Make bud from a small piece of green paste. Insert moistened, hooked length of 30 gauge wire. Dust with confectioners' dusting powder when dry.

12 Assemble and tape as shown with 2, 3 or 5 nuts in a bunch at the end of the stem and buds just above and below leaf.

Snowdrop

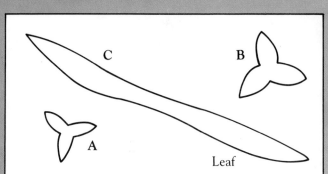

C

B

A

Leaf

THE shy bell-like flowers of the Snowdrop are welcomed as one of the earliest harbingers of Spring and have long been seen as an emblem of hope, bringing encouragement after the long, dark winter.

According to legend the Snowdrop became the symbol of hope when Adam and Eve were expelled from the Garden of Eden. During a snowstorm, the exhausted Eve could go no further and believed that winter would last forever. In the depths of her despair, an angel appeared and transformed some snowflakes into Snowdrops as a sign that Winter would soon be over.

It is believed that the Snowdrop was introduced into England from Italy in the fifteenth century. It is known to have been used by monks at Candlemas, a feast of purification, when the image of the Virgin Mary would be removed and replaced by a posy of Snowdrops. Snowdrops therefore became the symbol of purification.

Latin name: Galanthus Nivalis
Place of origin: Europe
Season: Winter
Colour: White
Cakes: Winter, Wedding, Celebration
Language of Flowers: Hope
Emblem: Candlemas

TO MAKE A BUD

1 Make an elongated paste ball and insert moistened, hooked, 28 gauge green wire. Leave to dry 24 hours. Paint tip green with edible food colouring.

*2 Using cutter shape **B**, cut a petal. Ball and shape petal slightly. Moisten centre and insert stem. Fold petals around centre to form a bud.*

3 Mould a green cone and insert moistened stem to form the calyx. Cut freehand 2 very fine green leaves, moisten and place one on top of the other as shown.

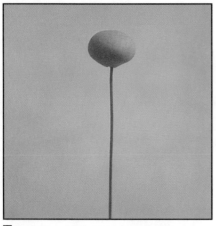

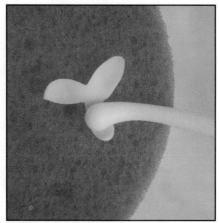

TO MAKE A FLOWER

4 Mould a ball of green paste. Insert moistened, hooked 28 gauge wire. Leave to dry for 24 hours.

*5 Using cutter shape **A**, cut and ball a petal. Slightly hollow out the centre of each petal as shown.*

6 Moisten centre and insert stem. Slightly close the petals up around the ball. Leave to dry for l hour.

7 Paint the tips of the petals with green edible food colouring.

*8 Using cutter shape **B**, cut and ball a petal. Hollow out the shape of each petal. Moisten centre and insert stem.*

9 Carefully fix the petals below the flower centre. Mould a small cone of green paste and insert moistened stem. Mould to base of flower to form the seed pod.

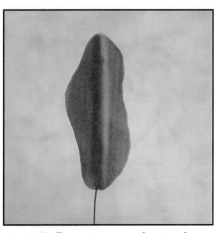

10 Cut freehand 2 very narrow leaves. Moisten and place on the stem curving over the seed pod. Bend stem to shape and tape carefully.

11 Roll out green paste leaving the centre slightly thicker. Insert moistened 28 gauge wire into centre of leaf.

12 Using cutter shape **C**, cut a leaf. Ball the edges and vein as shown (see p. 12).

Pansy

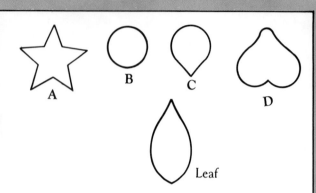

A   B   C   D

Leaf

ALTHOUGH the heartsease or wild Pansy is native to Britain, the cultivated Pansy is a recent creation. Old cottage gardens always had clumps of heartsease which were reputed to bring peace and tranquillity to the beholder.

In the nineteenth century, Lord Gambier, who had been ignominiously discharged from the Navy, took up gardening to forget his troubles. He employed a gardener, Mr Thompson, who created the beautiful 'faces' we know today, and who became known as 'the Father of Heartsease' due to his unstinting work in developing new species.

The delicate beauty and infinite variety of colours and markings make the Pansy a particularly useful and appealing flower for winter cakes.

Latin name: Violaceae
Place of origin: Europe
Season: Spring through to Winter
Colours: All shades of blues, purples, yellows and white
Cakes: Winter, Celebration cakes of all kinds
Language of Flowers: Thoughtful recollection
Emblem: Trinity Sunday

1 Make a small paste cone and flatten the base. Using cutter shape **A**, carefully cut a calyx.

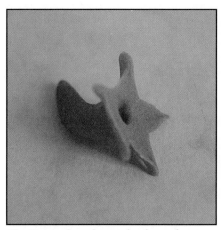

2 Curve the calyx to the shape shown and make a hole in the front with a cocktail stick.

3 Hook and bend a length of 26 gauge wire, moisten and insert into the top side of the calyx. Leave to dry for 24 hours.

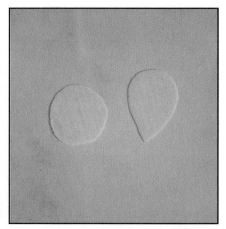

4 Using cutter shape **B** cut and shape a petal (2 required). Using cutter shape **C** cut and shape petal (2 required).

5 Moisten and fix 2 **B** shape petals to the top of the calyx.

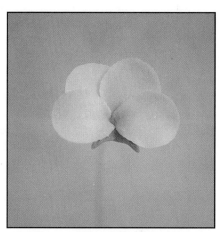

6 Moisten and fix 2 **C** shape petals to the left and right of the first petals.

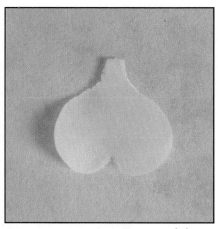

7 Using cutter shape **D**, cut and shape bottom petal.

8 Moisten and fix bottom petal into place. With the tip of a cocktail stick, make a hole in the centre. Leave to dry for 24 hours.

9 Paint centre and lines with edible food colouring. Dust petals to shade required with confectioners' dusting powder.

10 Pansies may be made in several different colours.

11 The 'features' of the pansy face can also be varied.

12 Petals can be coloured in 2 shades for variety.

Christmas Rose

THE Christmas Rose or Hellebore, which has black roots, arrived in England in the sixteenth century.

The Ancient Greeks believed that the hellebores were a cure for madness and this belief was still current in the seventeenth century when Gerard reported in his Herbal that it was 'good for mad and furious men' and those who were 'molested with melancholy'. The dried and powdered roots were taken like snuff and were also believed to ward off evil spirits.

In the medieval mystery plays, a country lass cries because she has no flowers to take to the baby Jesus. A kind-hearted angel is touched by her tears and causes the Christmas Rose to spring from the ground.

Latin name: Helleborus Niger
Place of origin: Southern Europe and Asia
Season: Winter
Colours: White, pink, green.
Cakes: Christmas and Winter Celebration
Language of Flowers: Scandal

1 Wrap fine white cotton round 2 fingers several times. Remove and twist as shown. Place very fine wire over the centre and twist to secure.

2 Tape the loops to 26 gauge wire. Trim the top and dip into yellow dusting powder to colour the tips.

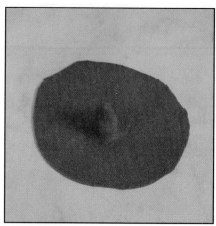

3 Make a cone from paste. Flatten the base with a small rolling pin.

4 Using cutter shape **B**, carefully cut a calyx and gently smooth the edges.

5 Insert moistened stem through centre of calyx and position stamens carefully.

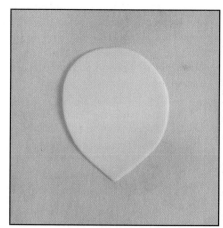

6 Using cutter shape **A**, make 5 petals. Cover with thin plastic.

7 Smooth and ball petal, lightly frilling the edges as shown.

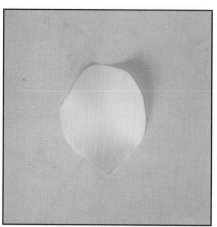

8 Colour the base of the petal with green confectioners' dusting powder.

9 Place petals on a former until the 5 petals are complete.

10 Moisten and fix petals on calyx as shown, slightly overlapping the bottom.

11 Position the final petal so that it lies over the previous petal and under the first petal.

12 Leave the flower to dry for 24 hours before use.

Jasmine

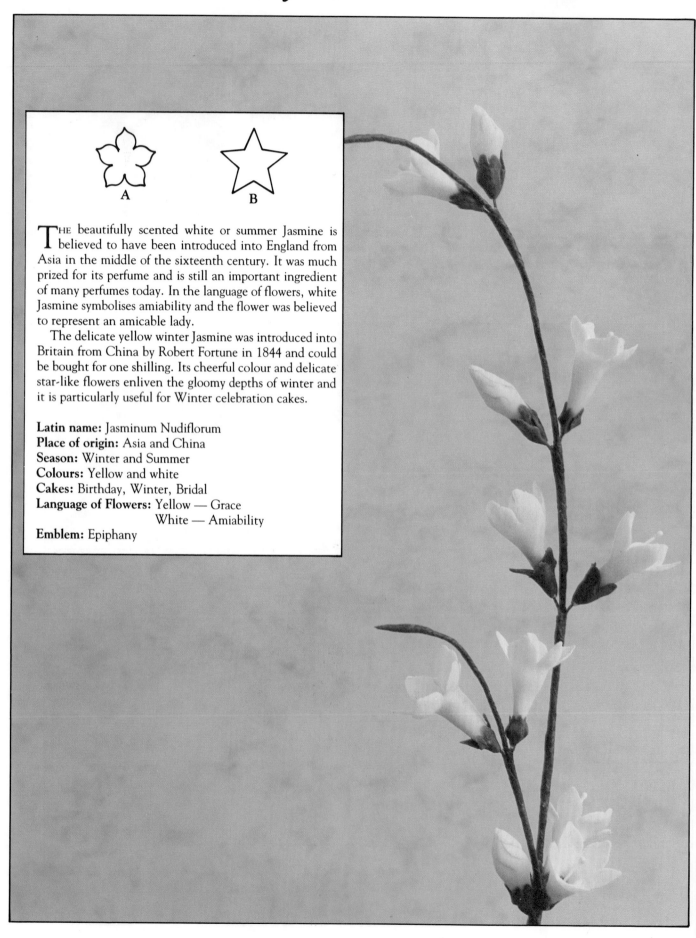

THE beautifully scented white or summer Jasmine is believed to have been introduced into England from Asia in the middle of the sixteenth century. It was much prized for its perfume and is still an important ingredient of many perfumes today. In the language of flowers, white Jasmine symbolises amiability and the flower was believed to represent an amicable lady.

The delicate yellow winter Jasmine was introduced into Britain from China by Robert Fortune in 1844 and could be bought for one shilling. Its cheerful colour and delicate star-like flowers enliven the gloomy depths of winter and it is particularly useful for Winter celebration cakes.

Latin name: Jasminum Nudiflorum
Place of origin: Asia and China
Season: Winter and Summer
Colours: Yellow and white
Cakes: Birthday, Winter, Bridal
Language of Flowers: Yellow — Grace
                             White — Amiability
Emblem: Epiphany

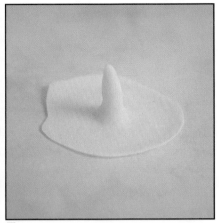

TO MAKE A FLOWER

1 Make a tall cone and roll out the bottom with a small rolling pin.

2 Using cutter shape A, carefully place over cone and cut a petal.

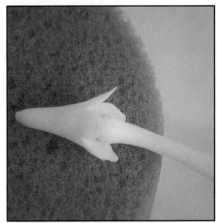

3 Gently ball the petals to form a slightly cupped shape.

4 Moisten and insert hooked 26 gauge wire through centre of flower.

5 Hollow out the centre of the flower with a cocktail stick.

6 Moisten and insert a yellow stamen in the flower centre as shown.

7 Using cutter shape B, cut a calyx.

8 Moisten centre of calyx and insert stem. Wrap calyx around base of flower. Leave to dry for 24 hours.

9 Tape flowers in twos and threes along a length of 26 gauge wire.

To make a bud

10 Repeat steps *1-4* as for an open flower.

11 Gently twist the petals together to form a closed bud.

12 Repeat steps *7-8* to form a calyx. Leave to dry for 24 hours. Tape to flower sprig at intervals.

Poinsettia

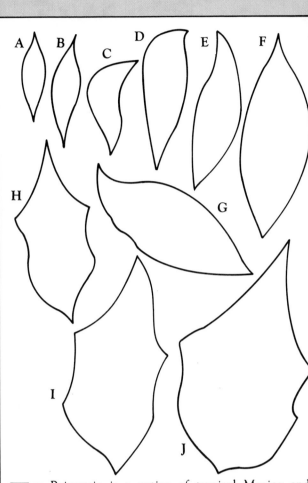

T<small>HE</small> Poinsettia is a native of tropical Mexico and Central America. A very popular plant pot in England at Christmas, the legend of the Poinsettia goes back to a Christmas Eve long ago.

Pepita was sad. This little Mexican girl wanted more than anything to give a fine present to the Christ child at the church service that evening, but she was very poor and had no gift. As she walked sorrowfully to the church with her cousin, Pedro, he tried to console her: 'Pepita', he said 'I am certain the most humble gift, given in love, will be acceptable in his eyes'. So Pepita gathered a bouquet of common weeds from the roadside and entered the church. As she approached the altar her spirits lifted, she forgot the humbleness of her gift as she placed it tenderly at the feet of the Christ child. A miracle occurred. Pepita's insignificant weeds burst into brilliant bloom. They were called Flores de Noche Buena— Flowers of the Holy Night. We call them Poinsettias.

Latin name: Euphoria Pulcherrima
Place of origin: Mexico and Central America
Season: Christmas
Colours: White, yellow and red
Cakes: Christmas

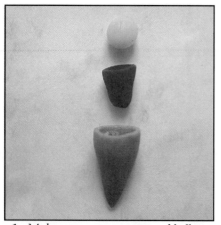

1 Make a green paste cone and hollow out the centre. Make a smaller red cone and hollow out the centre. Make a small ball of yellow paste.

2 Insert moistened, hooked 26 gauge wire into green cone. Slightly moisten and assemble remaining pieces as shown. (At least 12 stamens required, some with red centres).

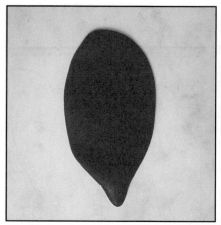

3 Make a large cone of paste and roll out leaving base slightly thicker. Using appropriate cutter shape, make 5 each of A-G petals. Cover with thin plastic.

4 Ball, shape and vein petals to appropriate shape (see picture 5). Insert moistened 30 gauge wire into base of petal.

5 Leave petals to dry for 24 hours.

6 Make a large cone of green paste and roll out leaving the base slightly thicker. Cut 5 each H-J shape leaves. Cover with plastic.

7 Ball, shape and vein leaves to appropriate shapes. Insert moistened, hooked 30 gauge wire into base of leaf. Leave to dry for 24 hours.

8 Tape 12 or more stamens together to form flower centre. Tape A petals around the stamens.

9 Carry on adding petals, increasing size on each layer.

10 Picture shows flower shape when red petals are completed.

11 Add the 5 **H** leaves to the flower. Continue to add the remaining leaves, increasing size on each layer.

12 The completed flower showing profile and position of leaves.

Index